IT DIDN'T START OUT THAT WAY

A WRITER REMEMBERS

JUDY BRIDGES

Hidden Timber Books
Milwaukee, Wisconsin

Bridges/Hidden Timber Books
6650 West State Street #D98
Milwaukee, WI 53213
www.hiddentimberbooks.com

Ordering Information:
Special discounts are available on bulk purchases. For details, contact the Publisher at the address above.

It Didn't Start Out That Way/ Bridges. -- 1st ed.
ISBN 978-1-7365519-6-7

PRAISE FOR IT DIDN'T START OUT THAT WAY

"Sometimes poignant, always illuminating, her insights will resonate with those who endeavor to live an examined life ...."

—SHAUNA SINGH BALDWIN, AUTHOR OF *THE SELECTOR OF SOULS, THE TIGER CLAW, WHAT THE BODY REMEMBERS*

"Judy Bridges' students have been waiting for this book. It is everything we knew it would be, and more than imagined. These stories are told with candor, heart, and humor when appropriate; quiet rage when deserved. This memoir is layered. On the one hand, it is a recollection and reflection of a life. Bridges makes you see people you have never met, yet feel you have. On the other hand, and even more magically, it shows how a writer transforms a life into art. On my bookshelf is Judy's *Shut Up And Write!*, an instructional book on the craft of writing. Next to it is a space for *It Didn't Start Out That Way*, the master's example."

—SHARON NESBIT-DAVIS, AUTHOR OF *INTENDED, A MARRIAGE IN BLACK & WHITE*, WRITING COACH, FACILITATOR FOR CREATIVITY RECHARGE WORKSHOPS

"With vivid detail and graceful prose, Bridges takes the reader's hand and leads them through a life well lived. From a childhood navigating two different households in two different states to her quest to find a sense of home, in place and in a partner—plus beautiful tributes to the relatives who shaped her along the way—this book sings with resilience and love."

—KIM SUHR, AUTHOR OF *NOTHING TO LOSE*

"If you're drawn to captivating stories (and who isn't!), consider yourself very fortunate to encounter Judy Bridges' memoir, packed with a lifetime of vividly described adventures, mindful observations, challenges, heartbreaks, celebrations, shared in riveting detail, akin to a cinematic rooming house bursting at the seams with fascinating characters of all kinds. Within the first few pages, I felt blessed that Judy invited me into her living room, where I wanted to stay and stay."

—HARVEY TAYLOR, MILWAUKEE ICON, STORYTELLER IN SONG AND POEM. AUTHOR OF LINES LIKE, "WHAT IF BIRDS REMEMBER YOU IN THEIR PRAYERS?" AND OF OVER 50 BOOKS OF POETRY

"Judy's voice is so appealing, you'll feel like she's your best friend, one who is smart, funny, and doesn't suffer fools gladly. In *It Didn't Start Out That Way*, you'll learn about the wacky characters in her very extended family, the men who abused her and loved her, and the not-so-good old days of the 1940s and beyond. Judy has set a new bar for memoirs, and it's a high one."

—CAROLYN KOTT WASHBURNE, NOTED FREELANCE WRITER AND EDITOR, ADJUNCT ASSOCIATE PROFESSOR EMERITA, DEPARTMENT OF ENGLISH, UNIVERSITY OF WISCONSIN-MILWAUKEE

"Who writes like this? 'The paper was yellowed and crackly, coming apart at the creases where it's been open and folded, again and again, each time breaking my mother's heart.' Judy Bridges does. On every page. I "luff" Judy, and I know you will, too."

—SARA RATTAN, WINNER OF SHORT STORY CONTESTS IN THE *WISCONSIN ACADEMY REVIEW* AND *GLIMMER TRAIN*

"Judy Bridges understands the way place can unsteady and shape us. Her stories reveal such atmospheric grace and understated power. Like the best writers, Bridges knows the exact moment to let wildness rush into each dazzling story and ruin us. Her entire collection sings with a complicated love for country, home, and family in these stunning stories."

—ROBERT VAUGHAN, EDITOR-IN-CHIEF AT *BENDING GENRES*, AND AUTHOR OF *MICROTONES*, *DIPTYCHS + TRIPTYCHS + LIPSTICKS + DIPSHITS*, *ADDICTS & BASEMENTS*, AND *FUNHOUSE*

"In her memoir, Judy Bridges reveals the big and simple truths of her life with gentle humor, the wisdom of distance, and incredibly humane clarity. Anyone who has ever sat down to write a sentence will appreciate the magic Judy conjures in stringing together captivating tales using language and images that are imminently accessible and feel real and authentic to the life of the writer. A story like "Husband Number One" becomes a tale of strength and empathy in Judy's hands, the marvel of someone telling a difficult truth of her own lived experience. I hope Judy lives to be 200 years old—it boggles my mind thinking about what she'd delight us with in a second volume.

—JONATHON WEST, WRITER, ACTOR, CONSULTANT, AND AUTHOR OF *MILWAUKEE'S LIVE THEATER*

Our life is a constant journey, from birth to death. The landscape changes, the people change, our needs change, but the train keeps on moving. Life is the train, not the station.

–PAULO COELHO

My dad's favorite picture of me. Mom went crazy with the hot-iron, trying to give me curls.

CONTENTS

WE ARE ALL BEGINNERS

After twenty-five years of coaching writers and leading workshops - and writing myself - I've come to one conclusion: We are all beginners.

I am often asked if a class is for beginners or pros, and foreheads wrinkle when I say it's for both. I love having a mix of people of different ages, genders, interests, and best of all, levels of experience. The person who has never put pen to paper sits next to one who is well published. High school dropouts sit with college professors, and factory workers with attorneys. Unless someone happens to mention it, no one can tell the difference. When we start writing, we all look alike. Each of us bringing the stuff of our lives to the page.

We write well one day and badly the next. We blow the grammar in one draft and correct it the next. We think we've nailed it when we haven't, and sometimes have it when we think we've failed. The truth is, writing is like life. When we're young, we imagine we're going to get smarter with experience and live on an upward curve, with our days getting brighter and happier all the time. Eventually we figure out life doesn't work that way. The happiness curve is a jagged line.

We begin anew every time we face a blank page. All the words in our heads wait to get sorted into proper order. But often, instead of flowing easily, ideas jumble, phrases bubble and then slip away. This happens to the pros as well as the beginners.

When we first started writing, we were sure it was all about inspiration, that lightning would strike with la grande idea. If we were to get out of the way, the right words would flow through our fingers to the page. All we'd have to do is let it happen. But writing isn't that easy. Work is involved. Even those "inspired" drafts need a lot of fixing.

Enter: Craft.

We take classes. Read books. Learn everything we can about the practical matters of structure, plot, character reveal, show and tell, point-of-view, dialog, etc. etc. etc. Surely now we are on the ascending curve to publication. We pay our dues, and the rest is going to be easy.

Ha! – says everyone who's been at this for a while. The blank page is still a blank page. You struggle to fill it with the right words, and you still need to do the fixing. With experience, you spot the mistakes more quickly and are more adept at revisions. But the path from word to sentence to page, is the same.

If you work in a single genre, you learn shortcuts, patterns you can follow. You begin with the murder, have X number of characters of one type or another, and XX number of plot points to cover. This makes it easier, but still there is that blank page.

You realize you are like every other writer on the planet who has to work to get it right.

Scary as that is, it's the good news. You wrestle with it. You write and re-write because your standards are high, you want it to be good. Instead of getting cocky you admit to feeling like a beginner.

And, if you are lucky, you'll be a beginner all your life.

IT DIDN'T START OUT THAT WAY

The Beginning. Dad, Mom, and Mom's Box Brownie.

Mom, please try not to move.

Where are we?

Emergency room. Saint Francis.

What happened?

You hit your head.

I couldn't move.

You were half out of it. On a back board for a while.

Take me home.

We need to wait for the tests.

I don't need any tests. See?

Mom! Don't twist your neck like that!

You'd think I fell off a cliff.

You fell on the floor.

How do you know?

I heard the crack all the way upstairs.

You have a big imagination.

The blood was pooled around your head like a halo.

That floor is slippery.

We could get it carpeted. What do you think? Blue? Beige?

Red. So the blood doesn't show.

Very funny.

How long did I lay there?

Until the ambulance arrived.

They're pretty fast.

They know the way.

Let's talk about something else.

Okay. Popcorn.

What?

How long did I stay with Marge and Leo?

A few months. What made you think about that?

You. On the floor. It reminded me of Leo.

Don't tell me I look like Leo.

You don't. One day Aunt Marge was gone, and I found him asleep on the kitchen floor.

Was he sick?

His mouth was open. I thought he might be hungry. So, I sat on the floor next to him and fed him my popcorn.

You could have choked him.

That's what Aunt Marge said.

I'm surprised you remember that.

I remember you sitting next to Dad when you came to get me. You were crying.

You wanted to stay with them.

I also wanted to go home with you.

They wanted to keep you.

Why was I there?

There was a while when I couldn't take care of you.

Why not?

Your dad and I were having trouble.

Must have been big trouble.

We came home from a party. He took the babysitter home and didn't come back.

Didn't come back?

I called everywhere. The police found them in a park.

Did they bring him home?

They kept him for a few days. He was on parole.

Dad was on parole?

From when he was in prison. Before I met him.

He was in prison?

It was that Dillinger thing.

You're making this up.

He and his up-north friends were robbing hardware stores and gas stations.

That's crazy.

Not that crazy. It was the Depression. People were hungry. The boys were like Robin Hoods.

That's hard to get a grip on.

Hard for you to get a grip on. You don't know what it's like to be hungry.

Where were you at that time?

Here in Milwaukee. I worked in a shoe factory. Stayed with Aunt Hazel.

You never got a break, did you?

I did when your dad came along.

Right now, it's hard for me to think of him as a great catch.

He was handsome. And smart. And kind. And generous. And he loved me.

Did you meet him at the shoe factory?

Sort of. He saw me come out after work and told a friend he was going to marry me.

Love at first sight?

I ignored him. Didn't want to tell him I was divorced and had Dorine.

I suppose that was pretty bad news in those days.

He came looking for me at the Eagles Club. I was dancing with my brother, and he cut in.

I thought he hated dancing.

Seemed to like it then.

Next thing you're going to say is that he liked to sing.

I wouldn't go that far.

What happened after that?

I came home from work one day and Hazel said he'd been there. He'd taken Dorine to the drugstore.

Did you panic?

Almost. I ran to the drug store and saw them sitting at the counter, chatting away.

That's a sweet picture.

Stole my heart. He arranged our wedding. Bought the flowers. And a beautiful dress for me.

Then you got your own apartment.

That was such fun. We bought a bed. A davenport. A set of pots and pans.

You had money.

Plenty of food. Clothes for Dorine. Your dad even helped my brothers when they needed it.

Where did he get the money?

He worked at an X-Ray company. Invented some machines. He was smart that way.

X-Ray.

That reminds me. We should be getting results on your tests.

Your dad was so excited when I got pregnant with you.

He wanted a boy.

He and his pals built a big iron bed for you. So big they couldn't get in the door.

That's funny.

He got me a special room at the hospital.

Ah yes, the front-window suite that belonged to the doctor's wife.

And he stood out on the street, waving up to me. Bringing flowers.

I'm sorry I wasn't a boy.

He loved you to pieces.

How long were you happy?

A couple years before you were born. Then another four or so. On and off after that.

He broke your heart.

He also broke his own. But I didn't realize that until later.

You're beyond gracious, you know.

I don't think he meant things to go that way. We just lost it, and we could never get it back.

Seems to me he screwed up quite a bit.

It didn't start out that way.

It never does.

Dad, me, and Mom's shadow.

THE TRAIN GOES BOTH WAYS

A car lover in the making.
Dad's Buick Roadmaster.

Dad bought the train when I was three. It was a Lionel with a big black engine and shiny tracks and a transformer that made it go fast – if you kept the tracks stuck together. When everything was right, when the Christmas lights sparkled, when there were no big lumps in the blanket surrounding the tree, the engine sped round and round, pulling a string of cars behind it. I put my head on the tracks and watched the engine barrel down at me, sure that Dad would grab me just in time.

My sister Dorine sat in the middle of her pile of gifts, wide-eyed and giggling. She was Mom's daughter by an earlier marriage – 13 years old and still not used to getting so many gifts. Gram detangled ribbons to save for next year. That was in the early 1940s. Mom, Dad, Gram, Dorine, Uncle Warren, and I lived in a big upstairs flat in Milwaukee.

When Warren joined the Army, Gram moved back up north, and we moved to a one-bedroom apartment on Milwaukee's north side. Mom and Dad slept in the bedroom. Dorine and I slept on a Murphy bed that dropped down out of the living room wall.

One day I sat on the living room floor playing with a twig I'd picked up in the field next door, switching it back and forth on the rug under the coffee table. Mom and Dad were sitting on the sofa, talking. I didn't understand the conversation, but I could feel the tension and wanted desperately to stop it. I broke my twig into two equal lengths, gave one half to Mom and the other half to Dad. I don't know what I thought they were going to do with their sticks, but I had the idea that if they each had exactly half, somehow that would solve things.

It didn't. When Dad got up and walked to the door, Mom followed him. When the door closed behind him, she leaned on it and slid slowly to the floor where she curled up in a ball and cried.

From then on, Dad was gone a lot. We never seemed to know for sure whether he'd be coming home or working late. I sat on the curb in front of the apartment, watching for his car to come down the street, hoping he'd stay home forever this time and Mom would be happy again.

In winter, when the streets were gray with slush, I'd buckle my galoshes, stuff our ration book into the bib of my snow pants and walk down the street to the butcher shop. I'd wait my turn in the line of babushka ladies, snow melting into a puddle around my boots, jingling the change in my mitten. When it was my turn, I held the wet mitten up over the counter so the butcher could take the money and wrap a small package of Mom's favorite Mortadella sausage for me to carry home.

If Dad's car was there, he might stay for a while, or take me with him for the day. Sometimes we'd go ice skating or drive out in the country to watch ski jumpers zoom down a rickety wooden ramp and fly into the air, leaning so far forward I thought they might crash and land face first. They never did.

One day he took me to the old Milwaukee Road station to look at the trains. I begged to go for a ride, by myself. I don't know where I got that idea, but Dad talked to some people in uniform, lifted me up to a porter and said, "I'll meet you in Chicago." He raced the train the 90 miles south and met me on the platform in Union Station. I can still see him walking toward me, hat tilted, a sort of half grin on his face. He took me to the Palmer House for lunch. I sat eye level with the tabletop staring at all the crystal and silver and didn't eat a thing.

When we got home, Mom was upset. "She's only four!"

Dad said I was nearly five and had to learn how to take care of myself some time.

Most kids had dads and uncles who were off to war – you knew because they had blue star flags in their windows. If a dad or uncle died, the blue star turned gold. At night, there were blackouts – we covered our windows and sat in the dark, listening for enemy airplanes.

Dad took flying lessons in hopes that the Air Force would overlook his ulcers and let him join. One day he said he had a special treat for me. We went to the airport, met his teacher, and before you know it, I was sitting in the seat behind the pilot, leather cap buckled under my chin, all in earnest, learning to fly. The pilot said to push this, pull that, and above all, do what he says. We circled the airport a few times, then headed "out to sea" over Lake Michigan. I was fine until he stared yelling, "Pull back! Pull back! We're out too far!" I pulled on the stick. Nothing happened. "Pull harder!" I pulled. I pushed. Nothing happened except my eyes got bigger. It seemed like forever before we turned around and landed.

It was a long time before I realized I wasn't really driving that airplane after all.

After Dad was turned down by the Air Force, he started a company manufacturing electrical parts – specifically, wire-round resistors he invented and made on equipment he also invented.

His plan was to keep the equipment and the plant small and special. When he shopped for space, he let me tag along. I pretended I was his sidekick, helping him get started. He played his part asking me what I thought of this or that and why.

One day we stood on the dusty floor in an abandoned tannery building, breathing the orange haze and tannery smells that filled the air from one bank of dirty windows to another. Dad pointed to where things would be – the furnaces, the long line of presses, the shipping department, the office. He turned his head toward rustling sounds coming from a dusty loft high up to our left. "It's a bum," he said. "He's been living up there. I'll have to put him out, but I hate like hell to do it."

I got to see the blueprints, and finally the factory all set up and running, just the way he said it would.

It wasn't long before I learned how to take the streetcar from my mom's apartment to my dad's new place at the Jackson Hotel. Also to take the train from Milwaukee up north to Gram's. I stayed with her a lot during those years.

The year I turned ten was so full of change a person could choke on it.

Mom and Dad divorced.

They each married someone else.

My big sister got married.

So did Gram.

Within a few months my family grew from four to eight. Nine, if you count Bob, the brother who came with mother's new husband.

Mom and I moved to Grand Rapids to live with my stepdad. All the way there, I sat in the back seat, hugging my goldfish bowl.

The house in Grand Rapids was dark and old fashioned. Mom felt as if Stepdad's first wife was still living in it. Still ill. Still unable to keep up with things. Mom started in my room – purple flowered wallpaper. New curtains. New bedspread. Then the kitchen – a soft yellow. Then the living room. Bob's bedroom, and the one that now belonged to Mom and Stepdad.

Bob took to Mom immediately. He loved her and she loved him. She made space in the attic for us to work on our model airplanes – tissue paper, balsa wood and a lot of smelly glue. Stepdad took us to a factory where they made plaster figurines. We came home with a shopping bag full of molds for grapes and sheep and dwarfs. We painted the figures and sold them to benevolent neighbors.

One sweet memory I have of this time is the way my brother and mom braided my hair. I sat on the tall chair in the kitchen, Mom on one side,

Bob on the other. They each brushed and braided, first the small braids at my temples, and then the long ones that fell down my back. They always, every time, came out even.

I tried to be nice to everyone, but I wasn't always able. One weekend a month and every vacation I boarded a Capitol Airlines plane and flew from Grand Rapids to Milwaukee to visit my dad. He remained my favorite, but I quit liking his new wife. She thought I ought to obey her. I thought I already had enough people to obey and said so.

I rolled my eyes at Mom. Stuck my nose up at the 25-cent allowance Stepdad thought was generous. If shrinks had been popular then, Mom would have taken me to one and thrown me through the door. But they weren't popular, and neither was Doctor Spock. If my folks were concerned, they didn't show it. They just kept expecting me to behave.

Years later and at different times, both Mom and Dad apologized. They said they didn't know how I survived the changes in schools and homes and parents. I said I had an advantage – nobody told me I was allowed not to. Nor was I allowed to feel sorry for myself. Though, I did, sometimes. But it didn't get me much mileage, so I quit.

I learned that the rule in one house was to clean your plate because children were starving in China. In another house, nobody seemed to think a clean plate would help them much. In one house you left the bathroom door open and in another you closed it. One day I got the signals mixed and led a troupe of girlfriends into the bathroom where my stepdad sat, looking stunned.

He had a hard time adjusting to having a girl in the house. I think when he first saw me, he expected to get braids and dresses. He got the braids. And blue jeans. And a daughter who was training for the wrestling team. He also got the tears when I didn't make the team.

When I decided to take baton, he bought one for me. In return I accepted more of his Croatian culture, which is to say, I started eating Sarma without holding my nose.

At Mom's house we went to church on Sunday. At Dad's we had friends in for brunch. Stepmom liked to dine in elegant little tearooms. She took me to Smartwear and taught me how to dress her way. When I mimicked the way she walked, she told me I needed to wait a few years – what I had wasn't worth swinging.

By the time Mom and Stepdad moved from Michigan to Ohio, I was beginning to grow up.

Dad would call from Canada or Florida and say, "Put her on a plane." I had my own suitcase – brown leather in a herring-bone pattern, with a snappy little lock. It never took me long to pack.

I didn't realize that I was living in a department store full of ideas. Each person had his or her own way of looking at things, of dressing, of manners, of coping with problems. There were Republicans, Democrats, Independents, and people who didn't bother to vote because they didn't think it mattered anyway. They had interests they talked about. They each took me to places the others would never have dreamed of taking me.

I saw the insides of factories, caves, barges, submarines, icehouses, whiskey stills, and segregated bathrooms in the South. One Christmas, when I was about twelve and on my way from Mom's home in Cleveland to Dad's in Milwaukee, the plane landed in Detroit. The pilot said there was a storm in Milwaukee, Mitchell Field was closed. He was going to try to get into Minneapolis; we could either go along or get off in Detroit. I got off. The plane was taxiing down the runway before I realized my stadium boots were still on board. I went to the ticket counter. Yes, they could send my boots into Milwaukee the next day. Yes, the Chicago field was still open. No, they didn't have a flight to Chicago.

I cashed in the other half of my round-trip ticket, walked over to another airline, and bought a ticket to Chicago. In Chicago I took a cab to Union Station. From there I took a train to Milwaukee.

I was surprised when I got into the Milwaukee depot, and no one was there to meet me.

I'd forgotten to call home.

I worried that Dad would be upset about me not calling, but all he said was, "I thought I taught you better than that." In later years I overheard him bragging to friends, but he never said as much to me.

I used to wish I had an ordinary family – with just two parents and real brothers and sisters, and friends I knew since kindergarten. But that's not the kind of life I had, and I've learned to like this other one. I got to know a lot of people, their good sides and their bad, and how they coped with this and that. When I get troubled, I can root around in my past and remember something somebody did, some time, that helps me get a grip on things.

And anyway, the more years that pass, the more I realize that one way or another, we're all on this train together.

SNOW, SNOW, BEAUTIFUL SNOW

Winter of 1947. Eighteen inches of snow in Milwaukee. The windows behind me are on the 2nd floor of our apartment.

My mother stands at the window, smiling out at the flaky stuff. I am three years old and already I've acquired the love of snow from her. Our sing-song voices share the joy, and it's years before I give it any thought.

This small moment in my life got bigger a few years ago, when Mom died, and I was going through her papers. I'd given her a three-ring binder to make notes of things she remembered. She filled the pages with penciled memories of pressing her brothers' pants for a penny, of dressing up in her big sister's flapper clothes, and of helping out the fancy lady who lived next door. And on one page, an entry about her dad standing at the window, singing, "Snow, snow. Beautiful snow."

Until I read that, I didn't know our snow love was a generational thing. If I got it from my mother, and she got it from her dad, did he get it from his mother or dad? And did they get it from their parents? For how many generations have my ancestors been welcoming snow?

On other pages, Mom remembered sharing bowls of potato soup during the Depression, going to dances with her friends, and marching with the Gray Ladies on the Fourth of July. In her written memories, I found my younger mother, the one I was too little to understand. It would not have been easy for my mother to write her memories. She was an avid reader, but having to quit school at thirteen left her self-conscious about her grammar and spelling. Words like 'ridiculous' turned into 'ra-dac-a-lus', and 'arthritis' into 'arthur-itis.' On top of that, her hands weakened in those last days so that it was hard for her to hold a pencil. And yet she filled page after page with things she wanted me to know.

I think of Mom when I get tired of writing, when the words won't come and my fingers ache. I worry about grammar, vividness, point of view, accuracy, and grace, when I should be taking a tip from her and just getting the words on paper. I should write what I think, say what I want to say and fix it later – or not.

The heart of writing, the only thing that really matters, is that we communicate. For some things – a published work, for instance, we need to polish to perfection. But for the written gift, the messages written for children and spouses and friends, all we need is ourselves – our imperfect, word-scrambling, ordinary selves remembering a man looking out a window on a winter morning, singing, "Snow, snow. Beautiful snow!"

REACHING FOR DORINE

Mom, Dad, Dorine, and me.
I am literally reaching for Dorine.

Mom's note on the back of the photo says it was taken the day I was baptized. My dad is holding me. I am six months old, leaning over, reaching for Dorine. She made her first communion the same day and was all dressed up in a new white dress, white shoes, white stockings, and a pretty white veil. For a kid who had nothing at all the first eight years of her life, that must have been quite a day.

Mom was just seventeen when Dorine was born. To save for the birth, she worked long, sweaty hours in a city diner. She hid the money for fear her husband would spend it on whiskey. By the time she and the baby were ready to leave the hospital, it was clear that he had found it. She had nothing. Nothing but a baby she would have to struggle to feed and clothe – but that was far from "nothing" after all.

The day he broke Mom's jaw, she took the baby and all she could carry to her mother. There wasn't much money there either, but it was better than being hurt, or worse, watching her baby get hurt.

In 1929, there were no homes for battered wives, and precious little sympathy for single mothers or divorcées. Mom had to pretend she was single to get a job or a place to stay. In order to earn enough to feed her baby, she had to pretend she didn't have one.

As the Depression deepened, Mom and Dorine stayed with Mom's brothers and sisters, other relatives, and friends. Mother and daughter were always welcome, but no one had enough money to keep both of them for long. Dorine slept in dresser drawers and bathtubs. Mom stayed in cheap rooming houses and moved from job to job, using what little she earned to pay for her daughter's care.

Dorine grew from a curly haired toddler to a shy little girl who missed her mommy terribly. One day she told a friend about her pretty mommy, that she lived in a big house and loved Dorine very much. The two girls walked a long way to a house with a steep stairway. They stood at the bottom of the stairs, calling up for Dorine's mommy. An angry looking lady came to the top of the stairs and said, "Oh, For Mommy." Then Mom looked down at Dorine and said, "No, she's not mine. I don't have any children."

In later years, both Mom and Dorine talked about that day. I could see the regret in Mom's eyes, the way she looked down, bit her lip. She knew the hurt she couldn't help but cause. Dorine understood. Mom would have lost her place to stay, and probably her job, if she admitted to having a child. But still, the pain of that day was deep and everlasting for both of them.

By the summer of 1937 the Depression was lifting. Mom and Dorine were together, staying with Mom's best friend, Aunt Hazel. Dorine was still sleeping in the bathtub, but there was food. And peace. And quiet. Mom had a steady job at the shoe factory, earning enough to save for a place of their own.

One day, as Dorine sat on the front steps tracing the grain in the worn grey wood, a man came up the walk and asked for Margie. Dorine said Margie was her mother, that she'd be home soon. Aunt Hazel came to the door, said, "Hello, Lionel" and yes, it would be fine if he took Dorine to the corner drugstore for a soda while they waited.

Mom was alarmed when she got home. She remembered being introduced to Lionel, even sharing a dance with him at The Eagles Club. But she didn't know him well and had not told him she was divorced, with a child. She hurried to the drug store to find the two of them siting at the counter, chatting away like old friends.

Before long there was a wedding. A new place to live. A real bed for Dorine, plus a warm winter coat with a matching hat. There is a picture of her

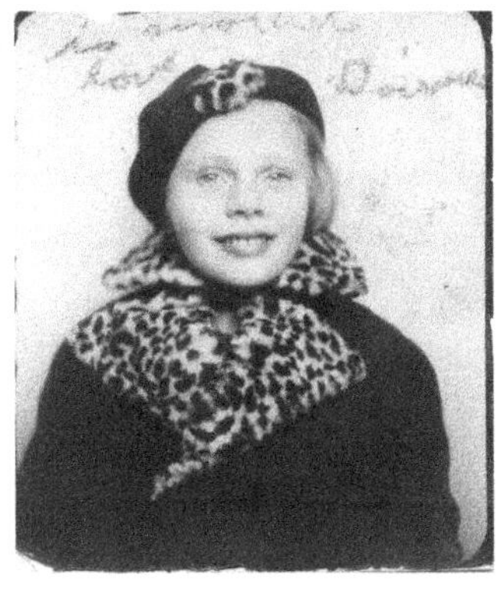

from a dime store photo strip. Such joy on her face!

And there was more to smile about two years later, when she turned ten. That's when she got a baby sister of her own to love. Love is the right word because that is what Dorine was all about. She was born with – and held all her life – the capacity to love, no matter the circumstances.

She took possession of me from the first day. She held me, fed me, showed me off to the old ladies who lived next door.

Where she was full of love, I was full of life. If she didn't keep an eye on me, I'd be off down the street, talking to strangers. Dad hung a sign on me, "Don't kiss me." No matter how much attention I got, she seemed to think I deserved it. That wasn't fair, and something in me knew it even then.

There was a huge shift in our lives later when Dad went away. Dorine was fourteen. Dad left and came back. Left and came back. Everything was askew. Mom cried and cried, for years it seemed.

Dorine was quiet for a very long time, until we moved into a nice apartment on 53rd Street where she made friends and became a regular teenager. I straggled behind her convinced that everything she did was wonderful. One evening, she and her girlfriends taught me how to smoke. I thought her report to Mom about my green complexion, "She's probably got the flu," was so brilliant I faked flu for days.

Dorine took up the violin. I hated the screechy sound it made. She chased me around the rooms of our apartment, screeching away, both of us laughing. It was funny until the night she dreamed I died and was buried in her violin, my little face framed in the round hole behind the strings. That ended her love affair with the violin.

She lipsticked, "Kilroy Was Here" on the hallway wall.

She cut the sleeves off her sweaters to make bobby socks. Mom stood at the door to our room. "What on earth were you thinking?"

Mom bought her a green army jacket with a fur collar. Dorine wore it with a pencil skirt so tight she couldn't take a full step. One day she tried to run away from some boys who were bedeviling her. Her skirt ripped straight up the back. I was right behind her, doubled over, laughing. She didn't think I was so wonderful then.

One afternoon a boy she knew tried climbing up to our apartment on the crossed bricks at the corner of the front porch. She yelled for me to get a pot of water which she dumped over his head as he climbed. Head soaked, he fell down, tried again, and finally gave up.

She used her baby-sitting money to buy me a set of "Alice in Wonderland" records. The album had a blue cover. I played it over and over until the cover frayed and I felt that I, like Alice, was falling... falling...

The last year of high school was awful for Dorine. Dad was coming home less often – only for holidays, or if Mom said I was sick. Mom thought if we lived nearer to his factory (he had a thriving business by then), maybe he'd come home more often. She moved us suddenly, not thinking about Dorine entering her senior year. Dorine was suddenly swept away from her friends. She couldn't seem to make new ones or build anything that would feel like a new life. She quit going out. Quit going to school. Quit everything. There was no turning back. She got a job at the cookie factory, at the end of a packing line that went too fast for her. When the boxes piled up, she ran off the floor and out of the building. She didn't stop to quit her job, she just ran. She walked around downtown all that day and finally asked a cop for streetcar fare to get home. She told Mom she would never ever work in a cookie factory again.

Somewhere in that lonely time she met a boy named Reggie. He was her first and only love. They were sweet together, dancing, staring into each other's eyes. He taught me how to jitterbug and gave me change to, "Go buy a comic book, and don't come back until you've read every word." I obeyed, but there was that time at the park when they were under a blanket making noises I didn't understand until later.

Suddenly, it seemed to Dorine and to me that the long back-and-forth of Mom and Dad was over. They divorced, he re-married and Mom started dating a new fella. She, the new fella, his son, and I all went to a cabin on a lake near Iron Mountain, Michigan. New Fella proposed marriage, saying, "Now or never." Mom reasoned that he was good with her girls, and we should really have an at-home father. They took his son and me to the County Court House and we became a brand-new family.

When we got back to Milwaukee, Dorine was in bed, crying. Mom checked. Cramps? No. What then? She broke up with Reggie. Why? She was pregnant. What did Reggie say about that? Dorine hadn't told him. Mom called Reggie – said he should at least know. He said they were going to get married, anyway. Just not so soon. The church, the dinner, the dress – arrangements were made in no time. Our aunts got together in the kitchen, sliced onions, made Sloppy Joes and lime green Jell-O molds. New-Fella was now Stepdad. He paid the bills.

When Dorine got near to having the baby, she started fainting. The doctors didn't know what was wrong until after the baby was born and Dorine went into a coma. They diagnosed Diabetes and didn't know for sure that she would pull through. Mom and I were living in Stepdad's house in Grand Rapids by then. She went back to Milwaukee to take care of Dorine while Stepdad stayed in Grand Rapids with Bob and me. When the new mother was upright again, we all got together in Milwaukee for the baptism. At ten and eleven Bob and I became the godparents of an adorable little girl we very nearly dropped into the baptismal font.

Also at ten, I started my periods. This belongs in a Dorine story because she was there, saving me when I thought I might die. I sat on the toilet, bleeding into the bowl, sure my guts were falling out. I can see me from her point of view as she sat on the edge of the tub and tried not to laugh out loud at this skinny little thing, all braids and eyeballs. She got herself under control and explained what was going on, a lesson no one thought to give a kid my age.

For Dorine and Reggie, life was all too much, too soon. They were barely out of their teens. Neither had great role models for a happy marriage. They were dealing with a new baby, Type 1 (brittle) diabetes, and a shortage of both education and income. They had a hard gravel road ahead of them.

We moved from Michigan to Ohio and back to Wisconsin. Sometimes they lived with us. Other times we did what we could from afar. Aunts, uncles, and friends contributed. Everyone loved Dorine. Real Dad and Stepdad each hired Reggie for a time. Mom and I took food when we thought the cupboard might be bare, and often it was.

We carried five-gallon cans of oil for the living room burner that so often went cold. We fetched insulin. When Dorine hurt her back sledding with the kids (by now she had more than one), Mom took care of the family and Stepdad paid the bill.

Dorene fishing off the shakey pier at Jack Lake. All her life she dreamed of going back there.

It's amazing how much help is needed when there are children and the well runs dry.

They had a very good period when Reggie got a nice job in Illinois. They bought a house and made a nice life for their five kids.

I am skipping some things, good and bad, because this could go on forever. In the end Reggie found a new love and the breakup broke Dorine's heart. She was like Mom – one man forever. Dorine's oldest daughter, Janese, was married by then. The other four kids were still living at home the night Dorine got up from the dinner table, said she didn't feel well, and fell dead on the bedroom floor. She'd been to the ER twice in the weeks before, suffering chest pains. They sent her home with a heating pad.

Our aunts summed it up at her funeral. "If there are angels, Dorine is one. She was so good, and she never got a break." Her kids are all grown now, old enough to retire. Two are married. Two are single. One died all too soon. I can tell when they visit their mom's grave because they leave pennies in the space inside the D for Dorine. A sweet hello.

Me? I want to feel the security of that day on the front steps, when she was dressed in white, and the world was all okay. I reach out to her often. "Let me touch you, my dear Dorine. You were the best big sister ever. I can never say goodbye to you, Dorine."

Dorene, age 17.

SANTA'S BEARD

I wasn't sure about Santa Claus. The Easter Bunny was *it*, the real thing as far as I was concerned. I hid under the Murphy bed in our living room and waited for the bunny to come. I never saw him, but one time he came and left a doll house full of furniture and a teeny tiny baby in a crib.

Santa didn't bring gifts like that.

I got gifts at Christmas, but they didn't come from Santa. Dad would arrive kind of late Christmas Eve and take me with him to buy a tree that was too big to get into the living room. While he sawed off the extra footage, Mom brought presents from her hiding place in the closet. When the tree was up and the Lionel train running around under it, Dad brought gifts in from the trunk of his car.

Gift opening was a quiet affair.

By that time, he and Mom stopped talking.

All I wanted that year was a German Shepherd. I did not want a picture of a German Shepherd on the face of a wind-up music box. I still have that buried in a bin with my baby bunting and dirty-toed shoes. The music box still works. Had I known what a metaphor was, I'd have understood why I saved it all these years. It was a not-quite-real gift. Semi-thoughtful. The giver knowing what was wanted and giving it halfway. Less than half, really. I guess it was the best he could do.

I was sure this Santa, the one at Boston Store, would do better.

I wanted to know if his beard was for real.

I asked if I could touch it.

He said, Yes. If I was very careful.

THE BOBCAT

My first best friend was my dad's mom, Eva, whose real name was Gram. That's what I called her and that was her only real name, just like the only real place she lived was "Up North." Dad's car knew the way there. I would ride with him, often late at night when the farms along the way had a single light burning in the barn, and parking lots at the roadside bars were empty. The door to Gram's log cabin was always unlocked but Dad knocked anyway, and after a bit Gram would come in her robe to let us in. She didn't say much, just took me to her bed where it was warm, and the grandfather clock wouldn't dare come to get me.

In the morning, Dad would leave, and Gram and I would settle into the routines of people who live in log houses on long dirt roads. She'd fire up the wood stove. I'd sit at the table, fingering the flowers on the oilcloth cover, watching her jiggle the iron burner tops off and on the round holes in the stovetop, poking heat from where it was to where she wanted it to be. Bread loaves rose on the overhead shelf. Raspberries wrapped in a cheesecloth cone hung from a hook on the shelf, dripping red juice into a pan on the stove.

We ate oatmeal for breakfast. Then walked down the dirt road to Ludwig's farm to find eggs. That was my job. It wasn't hard because Ludwig slept in the barn and left his shack to the chickens. They laid eggs under everything in and around the place, and I was short enough to see them. In no time my basket would be half full and we'd be on our way to get milk from Old Eddie.

Old Eddie's was halfway back to Gram's. Best to stop there last because we got milk in a small pail that could spill quite easily. We'd fetch the milk from the milk-house, which wasn't a house at all, just a lean-to space on the cool side of the barn. Eddie's house wasn't a house, either. It was a shack half the size of Ludwig's and just as messy. I don't know why I liked the place because nowhere I ever lived was that messy. But there was something about Old Eddie that made his shack feel warm.

I don't know whether these two old bachelors were friends, though they certainly cooperated with each other. One night I woke up alone in bed.

I could hear Gram at the door saying, "A buck? I can't imagine. Hanging in the pump house? Surely you don't think an old lady like me could hang a deer from the ceiling?" I kinda thought she could, but the warden let it go and we went back to bed. In the morning, Ludwig and Old Eddie showed up at the door and for the rest of the week Gram canned venison in rows of blue Mason jars.

Over time, Gram lived in a lot of places, but the whitewashed log cabin was my favorite. It had flower boxes and a big garden, but no electricity. No running water. We carried buckets from the pump house to the kitchen to wash dishes and faces. On laundry days, we poured water into washtubs set up on an old bench near the house. In winter we carried it to the basement and filled the washtubs down there. At first, I carried a quarter pail. Then a half. Gram always carried two full buckets.

My job was to turn the handle on the wringer. Gram scrubbed shirts and sheets on the washboard and rinsed them in the cleanest tub of water. Then she pushed them my way, to run through the wringer. I don't know what she did when I wasn't there.

I don't remember Gram baking cookies or making big meals for the two of us. I didn't like to eat, and she didn't threaten me like others who said I wouldn't get dessert if I didn't clean my plate. She knew I didn't want dessert anyway. She also knew my toothaches weren't real. And that I liked wandering the woods alone. And that I loved the smell of the barn that was full of hay even though it hadn't been used for cows for a long, long time.

When she took a break from chores, she would sit in her little blue rocker – it was smaller than the other chairs – and purr while I brushed her long hair. We both wore braids then, hers wrapped over the top of her head, mine tucked in the back pockets of my jeans. Hair washing and baths meant carrying more water, except in summer, when we walked to the lake.

Jack Lake was a couple miles down the road. Aunt Claire bought a cottage there on a land contract when she was just 17. It sat empty most of the time. Just us and the whippoorwills and whatever animals were around. We bathed in the cold spring water and cuddled up on the shore, a grandma-warmed blanket wrapped around us. We snacked on bread and berries, and no more than I wanted.

Raspberries were a big thing. Gram loved to pick and insisted everyone else go with her. If Mom or Dorine or Aunt Claire or anyone else at all was visiting, they were outfitted with long sleeved shirts, ties to wrap around pants legs, kerchiefs to cover hair, and rope handled pails to tie around their waists. I was valuable because I was little enough to pick the berries under the bushes, and also because I didn't eat half my pail-full the way some adults did.

The berry pickers: Warren's girlfriend, Warren, Mom, Aunt Ethel, and Dorine.

Blueberries were another thing. Gram picked those mostly in bogs and preferred to have people with her who were light-footed enough to skip over the swampy spots. Men seemed to have an especially hard time with this.

Uncle Marvin's dad was one of them. He visited often when no one else was around. His name was Henry, which Gram turned into "Heinie" and a little song and dance she usually did in the kitchen, swaying side to side in her housedress. "Heinie, Oh Heinie, I luff but you. No one could cut our luff haff in two."

One day when we were out in the bogs, she and I skipped ahead; he could not keep up. She found a small solid patch and stood there, looking back at him. "Heinie, Oh Heinie, I luff but you."

Heinie just shook his head.

Gram talked a lot. If we had visitors, she talked to them. Otherwise, it was me. I got so used to the sound of her voice I would miss it when she went to sleep. When she was mad at someone, which she often was, she'd walk around all day giving them hell about something they should have done and didn't or should not have done and did. She told me who married who when they didn't have to after all and really shouldn't have. And the real reason why those people down the dirt road had all those kids who were funny in the head. And whose hand that might have been that showed up near the railroad track with no body attached.

I know people think it's strange to tell a kid stories like this. But I loved hearing them. And I learned things – like, life isn't always nice, and you can't always fix it.

Evenings were good story-telling time. We'd light the kerosene lamps – so pretty with their hand painted flowers and soft, flickering light. She'd cover her legs with a crocheted lap robe, tap her foot to rock that little blue chair back and forth, and tell me how she met my grandfather. She and Chauncey worked in the hotel and logging camps his mother owned. He supervised work crews. She baked hi-brimmed pies for lumberjacks who sat at long wooden tables and called for more.

Gram was 16 when they married. Chauncey was in his twenties, newly diagnosed with consumption which he didn't believe, and she didn't know about. Before long they had two little boys they tucked into bed in a series of log cabins that dotted the north woods during the logging years. Chauncey worked in the nearby camps except for the weeks he needed to set up new locations. Gram said she was not afraid to be alone until one night when she awoke to the sound of the boys crying and loud banging at the door. She picked up the rifle they kept in the cabin and shot through the door. The loud yell was familiar. She'd hit Chauncey in the pocket. That's what she said every time she told the story, "In the pocket." When he complained, she told him, "If you don't know enough to say, 'Honey, I'm home!' you deserve to be shot."

Still, she luffed him best of all. He was kind, worked hard, spoke gently. When logging slowed down, he went to work for the railroads, staying in the railroad TB sanitariums out west when he wasn't feeling well. I have photos of him standing in the open air with a group of gaunt men wearing Indian print bathrobes. When he felt better, he'd come home. After one of his times at home, Gram had a new baby, a girl she named Claire. The next time he came home she told him, "No more." She wasn't going to have another child with a sick man and the only way to stop it was to keep him out of the house.

The last time she saw Chauncey was a few months before he died, when he took a train from California to Wisconsin to see her and the kids. He was so ill that he rode on a stretcher in a boxcar and stayed in bed at Muirdale Sanitarium in Milwaukee. His oldest son, Roy, was in the army overseas, so he couldn't make it. My dad, Lionel, was 16 at the time, living away from home, still angry with his mom for sending his dad away. He got there, but I don't think it was much of a visit.

Gram brought Claire from Appleton to Milwaukee to see the dad she barely knew. He was so sickly by then Claire said she wished she'd never seen him.

Gram's second husband was named Holgar, which always sounded to me like the perfect name for a man you didn't want to have around. It wasn't a good marriage, more heat than happiness, Gram said. One good thing they had in their time together was a boy named Warren who grew up to be a favorite uncle.

Gram's kids were grown by the time I started spending a lot of time with her, so she was happy to have the company. My parents were happy to have me with her for weeks at a time, away from the polio that was rampant in the city, and, although I didn't know it then, out of their increasing line of fire. I got the benefit of many sunny days and cold nights with Gram. She chopped firewood. Caught fish. Grew potatoes to grate for potato pancakes fried in her iron skillet on that big black stove. I got to see the world through her eyes, and she didn't hold much back. When the snake ate my rabbits, she said the snake ate my rabbits.

It was my instinct to take care of myself, even when I was little. But there are times when the fight is out of your league. When the better part of courage is to stand still and let do.

The Bobcat

One summer day we walked the dirt road back to Jack Lake – usually a quiet walk warmed with the smell of field grass. We had no mission that I recall, we were just going to be there. We were nearly to Claire's cottage, in a stand of white birches and half-dead trees when suddenly we heard this wild, wild screeching, high-pitched and fierce, coming from the crook of an old gnarly. The screecher was a big cat, bigger than any I'd ever seen. It hissed and snarled and scared me wide-eyed. Gram grabbed my shoulder, threw me down to the ground behind her, and gave me a look that said, "You stay put!"

She bent down, made a pocket of her apron, and quickly filled it with stones. The cat snarled, moving its haunches from side to side as if it was ready to jump at us. At what seemed like the last second, Gram threw the first stone at the cat, hitting it hard. Gram held still. The cat didn't. It started wiggling again, ready to fly. Gram threw another stone, then another and another, fast and furious until the cat fell out of the tree. It lay still when Gram walked over to check on it. She came back, wrapped her arms around me and held tight.

I could feel the quivering deep inside her.

When she talked about it, she said that was a bobcat. People said it could not have been, there weren't any bobcats left in those woods. I didn't notice its color or the shape of its ears, but if Gram said it was a bobcat, it was a bobcat.

That was the way of our time together until the year I turned ten, when everyone – Mom, Dad, my sister, and Gram – got married and moved to new places. Gram moved in with Bert, the man with the nicest house up the road. She whispered that the best thing about him was that he was alive at both ends. It took a few years before I understood that. At the time, I thought the best thing was having a bathroom with a big tub and hot water. The not-best thing was knowing his first wife died in the bed they expected me to sleep in.

It turned out Bert really didn't have any money. His plan was to be supported by Gram's children, who had other ideas. Gram grew a garden full of corn, and that's all we ate for one whole season. When she decided it was time for a divorce she filed on grounds of adultery. You needed "grounds" in those days. Bert was proud of her charge and didn't argue.

Gram moved in with a lady friend and baked pies for sale in the little diner in Kempster. I took care of her when she was old and frail, but I couldn't be with her enough of the time. She died in a nursing home in Antigo when she was 94.

The last truly wonderful thing she did was throw a tabletop Christmas tree out of her room and into the hallway. The staff took that as a sign of dementia. I know she was just mad at the person who gave her the tree.

THE KIEFERT CLAN

While in Milwaukee, and sometimes up at Jack Lake, I got to spend time with my mom's family. I never met her mom and dad. His name was Frank, for Francis with an i, Kiefert. Her mom was Frances with an e, Ronkowski. Grandma Kiefert was ill for years with diabetes and/or cancer and perhaps the exhaustion of having ten children. She died three months before I was born. Francis with an i did come to see me, but mom wouldn't let him in the door. When he tried to push past her, she slammed the door on his foot. She said he was mean to her mother and the kids. Stories abound of things the boys did to avoid getting hit and how their wives dare not nudge them in the night. Mom remembered having to stand up on bars to sing for his beer.

He did have talents, though. He was an excellent carpenter, and he started one of the first moving companies in Milwaukee. I think he started with a horse drawn wagon, but the earliest photo I have is of F. KIEFERT moving a horse. He must have made some money with the company, but it doesn't seem to have it made it to his home. His boys carried pianos and later, full size refrigerators upstairs to apartments like ours. They eventually graduated to large vans with doors that read KIEFERT MOVERS – and kept the company in business for many years.

The Kiefert gift to me was a huge tribe of aunts and uncles and cousins – all kind, generous, and playful people. Summer Sundays meant picnics for the Kiefert clan. All of us kids would pile in the back of a Kiefert van, roll on the floor and swing on the ropes – something kids would not be allowed to do today, especially in a van that's moving with the doors flapping open. Our parents filled three or four cars lined up behind us, the uncles tossing innertubes from one car to the next and back again. As far as I know, no one was ever hurt, but we did almost leave Uncle Frank out on a lake one time when he fell asleep in an innertube and floated out of sight.

Whenever home or the world at large got shaky for any one of us, we knew where to go. Brothers, sisters, cousins, friends, all were welcome for a handout. It was no surprise to wake up in the morning to see a different batch of cousins sleeping on the living room floor.

Older members of the clan still miss the mock weddings our uncles used to perform. Uncle "Brides" wore mop wigs and, of course, balloons in the right places. The father-of-the-bride chased the groom. The preacher sprinkled holy water from a glass. The flower-girl's dress was so narrow you saw eight inches of skin under the shoelacing in the back.

I know for sure that the younger brides and grooms are embarrassed by our mock weddings.

They out and out told us so. They just don't know what they're missing.

One of the last mock weddings, performed for Uncle Dan and The Last Aunt Lillian on their 50th anniversary. The uncles were getting old by this time, so the youngers stepped in. This handsome officiant is my husband, Dave.

THINGS YOU DON'T SEE ANYMORE

Tin boats that sink in the bathtub
Dollhouses with real wood furniture
Real live Easter Bunnies
Santa driving the Christmas Train at Boston Store
Shoes Mom let you wear for Dress Up
Ladies fur coats piled so high on the bed that a kid could hide in them
Roller skates that clamped on and fell off on the sidewalk
Gold stars on windows where soldiers used to live.
Ice boxes
Coal chutes
The jodhpurs we wore at Joy Farm
A big Lionel train whizzing around the Christmas tree
Clothes poles: the reach everywhere, fix everything, forked sticks in everyone's back yard

THE SHOEBOX

The paper is yellowed and crackly, coming apart at the creases where it's been opened and folded, again and again, each time breaking my mother's heart. In the envelope with the letter, there are torn-up photos of my dad, his younger brother, and two women. I suspect the women were "guests" of Dad when he went west to console his just-out-of-boot-camp-and-lonely-as-hell baby brother. Dad must have taken the women with him. Maybe he thought they would cheer up his brother. Or maybe he was just in it for himself.

Mom didn't show me the letter or the photos. I found them years later, after she died, in a shoebox buried deep in her closet.

Notes on the photos say, "Red Rocks, Colo, Margie and Anna." My mom's name is Margie. But that's not my mom.

The letter is addressed to Mom. In it, this woman starts out, "You know the old saying about A Woman Scorned? I do and I'm so angry I want to make a little trouble for one that deserves it."

She goes on to say she was dating my dad. Now he's interested in another woman who works for him and is completely unsavory. Woman #1 wants my mom to help her get rid of Woman #2. In return, she'll keep Mom advised of all that ensues.

I always knew Dad was a cruiser. I didn't know the word for it, but I knew there was something wrong about the way he acted toward women and the way they reacted to him. I also knew enough not to tell Mom. They might have been on or off at the time, but still, I knew she loved him. She would brighten when he came home, and cry when he left. Kids, even little ones, get the message in that.

The shoebox wasn't exactly hidden, at least not forever hidden. She meant for me to find it, or she wouldn't have had other things of mine in it – like the wire thingy they put on my thumb to stop me from sucking it. The white baby shoes with loose laces and toes gray from crawling. A twist of ribbons. A poem by Ruth Mary DuBois clipped from a magazine. In the slim margin surrounding the text, she wrote this note to me: "I've kept this poem all through the years as it reminded me of you when you were a little girl with long brown braids that you so hated for me to comb."

Dark brown braids that shine in my hands.
Slip in my hands
As I plait them down to the rubber bands
And the bright red bow.
...
And feet impatient to go.

I'm caught in the moment, remembering how much I loved Mom and adored Dad and somehow held back from loving too much. I think I was wary of being caught in the tangle of how they felt about each other.

There were days when I was the happiest kid in the world, and more days when I couldn't figure out what was going on. Dad took me with him way more than most dads – fishing, train rides, days in his factory hiding under the desks, challenging the secretaries to find me. Mom told him not to take me to bars, but of course he did. I fed the juke box for "Begin the Beguine" and "Swinging on a Star." Sometimes the bartenders let me pour drinks. One night I fell asleep behind the bar. I woke up just enough to hear someone on the phone saying she'd tell Dad to take me home. He did. Eventually.

I didn't know what an alcoholic was then, but I did know I spent more time in bars than any other kid I knew.

Mom was sick a lot, and she thought I was, too. When my stomach hurt, she called Dad to hurry home, and he did. One time he beat speed records driving up north to where I was at Gram's, only to be told I'd eaten too much candy. I doubt if he believed that.

At one visit, Dr. Callan said, "Mother, there's nothing wrong with this child but her parents." Mom held it together until we got on the streetcar, and then she cried all the way home.

Might that be the day she received that ugly letter? I would not have known, nor would the doctor, how badly she was crushed. And if she didn't receive it that day, on what other day did she get smashed in the face with a reality she may have already guessed, or known, but certainly didn't want to see up close with photos and all. Was she crying because she was sick, or tired, or just fed up with everyone expecting her to give more than she had to give?

My braids tell a story of those early years. I had them since I was little – long brown braids worn loose or tucked in the back pockets of my jeans, until I spent a school holiday in Milwaukee with Dad and my new stepmom. She thought my hair would curl if it was cut. It didn't. When Mom saw me coming down the ramp at the Grand Rapids airport, she started crying. The silky braids that slipped through her fingers were gone.

That might have been when she tucked the Little Girl poem into the shoebox. I suspect the crinkled letter was already there, that the poem and the letter sat together for years – all that was left of a marriage gone sour, and a mom and a dad who tried hard not to go sour with it.

GOING TO HELL

Mom didn't know anything was going on until the principal called her in to talk. I was cutting school. Peculiar behavior for a 4th grader. The principal was puzzled and so was Mom. Whatever could cause me to do that? How did I manage it? Mom looked like she was going to cry. She kept repeating, "I don't understand." "I just don't understand."

I was too afraid of the principal to say anything at all. And once I was not saying anything to the principal, I couldn't talk to my mother, either. I was all one big knot inside.

I don't recall the name of the sister who taught 4th grade at Holy Angels. I do remember her standing in front of the room saying that divorce was a very big sin. People who divorced would go to hell when they died. That's how God punishes people who get divorces. Their kids go to hell, too.

Did she look directly at me? Did the kids look at me? I don't know, but it felt like they did. I do remember that some would not play with me after that. And there were parents who wouldn't let their kids play with me once they heard that sorry news.

I can't even say what I felt like. Lonely, I guess. Like an outcast, though I wouldn't have known the name for it. My stomach hurt. I didn't want to go to school. Mom got me off to school every morning, but by the time I came home for lunch she was gone to work. So, I just stayed home alone. Sometimes I played Mass, me being a priest who heard my own confessions and forgave all sins.

Someone gave Mom the idea that what I needed was a good spanking. The very thought must have chilled her. Two rules that she and Dad shared were "No Yelling" and "No Hitting." She looked pale when she told me to bring the wooden spoon, the one with the holes in it. She gave me one whack and broke down in tears saying, "I can't do this."

She called Dad. He was good at getting things out of me that Mom couldn't. He picked me up in his car and parked where it was quiet so we could talk.

At first, I was too smooshed to say much. When I did finally tell him what Sister said, he gritted his teeth. "They aren't always right."

We might not go to hell after all.

JACK BE NIMBLE

Me and brother Bob at the courthouse in Iron Mountain, Michigan, the day our parents got married.

The 5th grade girls are lined up on the playground, waiting their turn at Double Dutch. Two long ropes arch high between the turners. Jack be nimble... Jack be quick...

A girl runs in, braids bouncing over her navy-blue uniform, sturdy Buster Browns skipping over the ropes. Jack jumped over the candlestick... She calls the name of a friend to take over the skip. That girl calls another, and that girl calls another until all the girls have had a turn.

Except me.

No one calls my name because no one knows it. I'm the new kid in school. Again. St. Mary's Academy is my fifth school in five years, the fifth time I've walked up to a big brick building and into a room full of strangers. I have to start all over making new friends. I know how to do this, but this time it's going to be harder than ever.

Sister Evangeline introduces me, tells the kids I came to Grand Rapids from Milwaukee, says my new brother was in her class last year – such a nice boy, a good student, an altar boy. She says his mom got sick and went to heaven. She tells them my dad died, too. So, his dad married my mom and now everything is fine.

Only it isn't fine. My dad isn't dead. She thinks he is because my new brother said so. Before school started, he took me to the convent to meet the nuns. (Only an altar boy does that.) We sat in their stuffy living room, and he told them, plain as day, that it wasn't a sin for his dad to marry my mom because she wasn't divorced or anything, my dad was dead, too. I should have told them right then that my dad was alive and I go see him a lot. But I didn't say that, and now here I am in the classroom, and everyone is looking at me. They believe what isn't true, and I don't know what to do about it.

So, I shut up. All year. No talk about the airplane rides to Milwaukee, or the skates I got for Christmas. I don't tell that my big sister is pregnant, or that my grandmother just got married, or that I'm hiding new breasts under the two tee shirts I wear under my blouse.

Sister Evangeline hates that I can't sing soprano. She sends me out into the hall to think about it.

When she catches me writing backhand like the left-handed girl beside me, I say, "I always write like that," and have to keep doing it all year. I still write backhand.

The last day of school, I clear my throat and tell Sister Evangeline and the whole class that my real dad is not dead, he's still alive, and I see him all the time.

They just sit there, staring at me.

As I wrote those words, felt that moment, the memories reeled through my mind. New schools. New homes. How many were there?

Elementary and Middle Schools (9)

Kindergarten: A public school in Milwaukee. Mom is told to go away, so I'll quit crying.

1st Grade: Another public school. Staring out the window, imagining a day with dad.

2nd grade: Mother of Good Counsel. First Communion. Cinnamon sugar on white rice.

3rd grade: Holy Angels. Milwaukee. Paper drive. I feel useful.

4th grade: Holy Angels. Sister says divorced people – and their kids – go to hell.

5th grade: Saint Mary's, Grand Rapids, MI. I have a secret.

6th grade: Park Elementary, Chardon, Ohio. Maypole dancing. Boys exist.

7th grade: Wilbur Wright Junior High, Cleveland, Ohio. My shoes are ugly.

8th grade: Wilbur Wright Junior High. Lots of tough cookies.

High Schools (3)

Freshman & half of Sophomore: Pius XI, Milwaukee, WI. Sister Beatrix "got" me.

Second half of Sophomore year: Our Lady Academy, Manteno, IL. Macaroni every day.

Junior and Senior years: St Clara Academy, Sinsinawa, WI. A gift.

Colleges and grad school: (6)

American University, Washington D.C. Business. Philosophy. Writing.

University of Maryland, College Park, MD. Good at Nursing. Choking on Chem.

Montgomery County Community College. Nursing. Wanted to add computers. No dice.

Fairfax Community College, Fairfax, VA. Old Testament. Creative Writing.

College of Du Page, Glen Ellyn, IL. Creative Writing.

University of Wisconsin, Milwaukee. Bachelors: Business and Creative Writing. Masters: Writing. Administrative Leadership.

Total number of schools: 18.

Total number of homes: Sixty or more in the following places. Milwaukee WI, Grand Rapids MI,

Chardon OH, Cleveland OH, Rocky River OH, Westlake OH, Wauwatosa WI, Brookfield WI, Bowie MD, Silver Spring MD, Reston VA, Oakton VA, Bull Run Mountain VA, Elmhurst IL, San Francisco CA, Shorewood WI, Bay View WI, Waupaca WI, back to Bay View, and Waukesha.

No single reason for all the moves. Change just happens.

And then it stops. I fall in love with a cozy neighborhood in Milwaukee, buy a house, start a business, get married (for the third time), have lunch with the same friends for years. We don't jump rope. I don't think about moving until my dad's sister leaves me her home, a country ranch with huge windows and lots of squirrels for our dog to chase. I love the place, and it would be cheaper to live there, but the thought of moving again turns me into an idiot. Yes. No. Now. Later. I twist and turn and talk and talk and drive my friends nuts with my fussing.

I swear, I've gotten married with less consideration.

One day I'm standing in the kitchen, yakking about how I would miss my friends. "It's like starting a new school," I say, "standing out on the playground, watching the other girls jump rope."

And suddenly I'm in tears, feeling every lonely pain I felt when I was a kid.

My husband takes me in his arms. "We don't have to do this," he says, "not if it makes you this sad."

In that one minute, realizing what I was afraid of, I quit being afraid. I could think clearly. Get a grip on what I really wanted – To stay in Bay View. To watch the girls next door dance on our front porch. To know if I yelled for help, someone would hear me and come to help.

The dog will have to settle for city squirrels.

HOUSE KEYS

The summer after 5th grade, Stepdad threw a set of keys on the table and announced that we were moving. He expected glee and he got it. Mom had painted and papered every room in the old house in Grand Rapids and it still looked gloomy. She tried to be a cheerful newlywed, but she could not get used to walking through the bathroom to get to the kitchen. My brother was happily settled at St. Mary's. I loved him but hated school. I didn't have the words for it then, but I was struggling to find my place in a world of changing homes and parents and even ways to dress and which foods to eat. Would I learn to like my stepdad's canned peas cooked with bacon grease and vinegar? No! I sat at the table for hours until he finally gave up and let me go to bed. My few friends wanted to know how it was that I had parents and siblings living in different houses, in different cities, and what it was like to fly back and forth between them all the time. In the new house, wherever it was, I wouldn't tell anybody anything.

Happy first days in the cool house in Chardon, Ohio.

We moved into a big house in the country near Chardon, Ohio – a small town destined to become a snazzy suburb of Cleveland. Everyone but Step-dad loved the place. There were bedrooms enough for all of us. Mom and Dad. Dorine, her husband, and baby. My brother, Bob. And me. Mom loved the dining room with its French doors opening out to a sunny brick patio. Sister loved having beautiful places for her baby to play. Bob and I loved the buzzers in the kitchen meant to call maids who didn't live there anymore. And we loved the woods, where we let our imaginations fly. We hid from the bum we thought slept in the brush. We tiptoed across the creek on fallen logs – arms stretched out for balance – and belly-crawled up the hill to where we could watch gangsters going in and out of the estate on the downside of the hill.

In fall, we walked to the main road and waited for the yellow bus to what was more-or-less a country school. The farm kids got days off to help with harvest. I wore jeans and enough t-shirts and flannels to hide my growing breasts.

On May 1st, we danced around the Maypole. I wore a dress that day, and suddenly all the boys who wouldn't let me play baseball wanted me on their team.

The thing Stepdad didn't like about Chardon was the house. He picked it without noticing the old-fashioned furnace he'd have to feed. Twice a day, all winter, he had to walk out the back door, past the four-car garage, down the outside stairs to the cellar, and shovel the coal that heated the house. Bob wasn't big enough to help much. And Reggie just didn't. At least not often. Not even when he quit work and signed up for photography school. He'd have been good at that, but real men don't quit work, you know, no matter how good they are with a camera.

Me and Bob, 11 and 12-years old. Backlit by Reggie.

So one night, Stepdad came home with the keys to a house in the city. Again, he tossed them on the table and smiled and expected us to be thrilled. We were not. The room went cold and got colder yet when he said the new house was too small for my sister's family, that she and her husband would have to find a place of their own.

My sister and her husband were gone by morning – back to Milwaukee, they said, to start over again.

Bob and I quit hanging out in the woods. Mom still got dinner on the table on time, but the lady with the pretty voice quit singing.

Wilbur Wright Junior High School

Wilbur Wright Junior High was within walking distance of our house on 90th Street. Bob settled into classes – he was so good at that. For me, everything was crosswise. The girls at school didn't think much of me. My shoes felt so dumb I tried to walk with my feet behind me. I got Stepdad to buy me a pair of white bucks. He came down the stairs to the basement just as I was swiping furnace dirt from the sole of one shoe to the white of the other. I heard about that for the rest of his life.

A girl named Gloria was friendly until her boyfriend said I was cute. Then she grabbed me by the back of the neck, pulled my head forward into her knee and yanked out huge patches of my hair. That made it my turn. I picked a fight with a girl whose mom did me a favor by breaking it up while I still had some hair on my head.

From then on, I focused on the boys. First was Jerry Oriel, the cute guy down the street who could neck like crazy. His mom worried about us, but she needn't have. I was too chicken to go too far. Next came Ralph. I wrote a love note to him one morning. By noon I was in love with his cousin, Nick, so I wrote a note to him. I don't remember how I got my messages to them at the Jesuit school, where they were in the same religion class. Brother John saw what was going on and made them stand in front of the class and read my notes. Every word. Out loud.

Eeek.

The History teacher at Wilbur Wright kept a bottle of vodka in the bottom drawer of her desk and poured big glugs of it into her water glass. One day we put tadpoles in the glass, laughing at what would happen if she swallowed one. I don't think we really expected her to, but she did, and we sat agog as she spit watered-down vodka and tadpoles onto her desk.

There must have been good teachers at Wilbur Wright Junior High, but I don't remember them. I remember the Home Ec teacher who yelled at me for bleeding on her sewing machine the day I caught my finger under the needle. (I always was a bleeder.) Then there was the teacher who liked girls, particularly girls with lots of stuff up top. He'd get them writing on the blackboard and slide his hands around to where they shouldn't be. The boys watched as if they were taking lessons. Some of the girls snickered; others wished they'd be chosen. I was a wisher until he moved on me and then I wasn't anymore. Today you'd wonder why no one told on him. Truth is, it wasn't a big deal then. Certainly not in that school or in that neighborhood.

Kids in the neighborhood were either Irish or Italian, and I was neither. Tom Coyne was my best friend on the Irish side; Nick DiNardi was my favorite of the Italians. Neither Tom nor Nick were deep into the gangs, which was good thing, because the gangs were seriously tough. One gang would hang out on the flat top of a park building, waiting for the other, both troops snapping brass knuckles and billy clubs. One night the Irish boys pressed an Italian kid up against the schoolyard fence and jumped on his legs, breaking both of them.

By the spring of 8th grade, I'd had it with the tension at home and school. Two boys, a girlfriend and I decided we would run away from home.

We'd hit the road for Milwaukee where I would live with my dad, and they would do whatever. I cut afternoon class, so I could get home while Mom was still at work, crawled in through the milk chute, and packed my suitcase. The boys and I headed downtown to a shabby hotel room they had rented. The other girl had chickened out by then and told her mom what we were up to. The boys and I were sitting on the beds, reading "The Pit and the Pendulum" when the cops walked in.

They put the boys in one car and me in another. The lady cop with me kept asking questions. When did it happen? How many times? She had to get all the way to "Are you pregnant?" before I caught on. Pregnant? What the hell, we were reading a book!

And so began my three or four weeks in the detention home. My husband thinks this is so charming, he keeps referring to it as the time I spent in Juvey. It wasn't at all like that. Well, half of it wasn't anyway. At first, they were going to send me home. Home meant living with my crummy family and going to that crummy school. I said "No! I ran away from there and I'm not going back." They put me in the dorm with the nice girls, who were waiting for foster homes. I set my suitcase on the bed and unpacked my things. Skirts.

Blouses. Undies. My steam iron. Yes, my steam iron. And no, I don't have any idea why I'd taken it along. I don't even know another 13-year-old girl who has her own steam iron.

Next came the warnings. I don't know whether the girls in the dorm liked me or realized I was naive, but they were kind enough to warn me about The Doc. Intimate physicals were required. The Doc does them, alone with you, in his exam room. He makes you put your feet in stirrups and crams his fingers in you as hard as he can. If you're lucky, that's all he does. They didn't bother saying, "Try to relax." I couldn't have. He started. Got his fingers a little way in. Pulled out. Said he was sorry. And that was that. I didn't know what to tell the girls when I got back to the dorm. It didn't seem fair that I got out of it.

Next came the therapists. What was so awful at home? Did I realize my mother was heartbroken? My stepdad was angry. My real dad was asking for custody. His wife wrote a long letter saying how much she loved me. A judge would make the decision, but what I said would count.

I wanted to puke.

Right about that time one of the girls in the Bad Ass Dorm was making plans with one of the boys I'd run away with. She wrote a note to him and signed it with my name, not hers. I, of course, refused to tell who she was. That got me transferred to Bad Ass and a look at a world I'd never known. Very quickly the girls figured out I was a virgin, the only one in the crowd. One girl came after me in the shower. Another bigger one pulled her off. It turned out the bigger one was Queen of The Bad Asses. She decided to protect me, and I was sincerely grateful.

Step One of the Queen's escape plan was to break out a window, stick her fist through it and flip the lock. She did that, but as she pulled her arm back in, she dropped it a little and cut it from elbow to wrist. She wrapped something around the bleeding arm, ran for the elevator and pushed the button. The door closed once she was in, but it opened on another lower floor. By the time she reached Floor One, she'd knocked out two of the guards, injured a third, and was being held down by a fourth. It was all over. They took her to the hospital to take care of the arm – 122 stiches, I remember exactly. They kept her in solitary after that.

On one bright and beautiful day, I walked into the social room to see a lineup of girls facing out the window, making hand signals to someone on the street. When I joined them, I saw that the someone was a man leaning against a car, making hand signals back. He unzipped his fly and pulled out the longest dong I, to this day, have ever seen. The girls broke into awe and laughter. I made for the bathroom where I proceeded to puke. The guard came by. I heard her voice outside the door, asking, "What's the matter with her?" For the second time in my life, someone answered, "She must have the flu." They escorted me to the infirmary, which turned out to be a solitary room right next to my bad-ass friend. I was quite content to stay there for a few days.

When Real Dad arrived from Milwaukee, everything changed. By that time, I was crazy confused between Mom and Dad. I didn't want to hurt her, and I didn't want him to go home without me. Lawyers were involved. And a court room. And a judge. I heard my dad say, "I don't know what they're thinking having a girl her age in a neighborhood like that." I heard my mom's attorney say my dad was an alcoholic. Stepdad said something about all the money I was costing him. The judge read the letter my stepmother wrote, and my real mother cried louder, "She doesn't mean it! She doesn't mean it!"

The judge awarded custody to my dad. Mom and Stepdad very quickly bought another house in nicer neighborhood. She hoped that would get me to change my mind, but things were too far gone by then. In a month or so I was in Milwaukee and the only one I missed was Nick DiNardi. We kept in touch for a few years. He's gone to greener pastures now.

I still have the Poe book I took with me on my great escape. It's the collection Dad read to me when I was very young and fascinated with the rhythm of "Annabelle Lee" and the "tintinnabulation" of the "bells, bells, bells."

I also have a book of quotations from that time. The inside cover is stamped "Property of Wilbur Wright Junior High School Library." I obviously never returned the book. Every year or so, I thumb through the pages looking for quotes I checkmarked way back then.

> *"There is a certain relief in change even though it be from bad to worse; as I have found in travelling in a stagecoach, that it is often a comfort to shift one's position and be bruised in a new place."* Washington Irving, *Tales of a Traveler*

I knew what it was like to be bruised.

> *"Talent is nurtured in solitude; character is formed in the stormy billows of the world."* Johann Wolfgang von Goethe, Torquato Tasso

I grew up in "stormy billows."

> *"Live as long as you may, the first twenty years are the longest half of your life. They appear so while they are passing; they seem to have been so when we look back on them; and they take up more room in our memory than all the years that succeed them."* Robert Southey, *The Doctor Going to Hell*

I cherish, and cry for, the first half of my life.

THE INDUSTRIALIZATION OF LATIN AMERICA

Pius XI High School, Milwaukee, WI

Freshman and First Half of Sophomore Year

It's Freshman Year. I'm way out of time to write a paper that's due tomorrow. The topic is supposed to be something that interests me – one that I will enjoy researching and discussing in six pages. I rifle through my dad's bookcase looking for something I hope the teacher knows nothing about so I can pretend I actually got interested and did some research. There it is. The Industrialization of Latin America. Who else knows any-thing about that? I write like crazy. Finish it off two minutes before I fall asleep. I turn it in the next morning. The teacher picks my paper out of the pile. My heart stops. He reads the title: "The Industrialization of Latin America." He starts laughing. Out loud. He tries to tell the class why he's laughing and can't. He looks at me like I'm a total wonder and gives me a D.

That turned out to be my average grade in high school.

Sister Beatrix was the principal at Pius. She reminded me of a Bing cherry – round, red-faced, always looking like she might burst into something sweet and messy. She said I'd be welcome at Pius – as long as I behaved myself and kept my uniform pressed. I managed until the first day of gym class.

We were supposed to have our names embroidered over the chest pockets of our gym suits. I guess most moms knew how to embroider, but my stepmother didn't. I thought I'd have to go to class nameless until a friend whose class met at a different time loaned me her gym suit – with her name on it. We figured the teacher might not notice. I stood in a line with the other girls, head up, back straight. The teacher came along the row to me, looked at my face, looked at the pocket. My face. The pocket.

"What's your name?"

"Uhhhh..."

"Go to the office."

Sister Beatrix looked at me. Same question, "What's your name?"

"Uhhhh..."

"You obviously need help remembering your name." Her solution was for me to write it 500 times and bring the list to her office the next day. Perhaps that would make an impression.

I enlisted classmates who helped me fill page after page with row after bumpy row of my name – Judy Weyenberg, Judy Weyenberg, Judy Weyenberg. Next day, I put the mess on Sister Bea's desk, hoping she would not look closely.

She had a tiny smile on her face.

In retrospect – which is the only safe way to look at your high school years – I think Sister knew before I did that things were not going to work out well at home. Not only was I in a daze half the time, once a month I was sick in her office, curled on a chair, crying in pain. Dad would come to pick me up. He and Sister Bea would shake their heads, not knowing what to do to help me. No one knew much about endometriosis then. Doctors had differing solutions. Hot baths. Heating pads. Ice packs. Bed rest. Walk it off. Do backbends (no kidding).

My stepmother swore one of the doctors said, "Send her to Hollywood." Like I was acting.

I have to admit to being a lousy student. A last-minute crammer, bad at math. I was pretty good with word problems, though I couldn't say how it was that I knew the answers. I could read blueprints and figure out how machinery worked, but those skills were not particularly useful in high school. I also scored high on IQ tests, probably because of the extra practice I got when teachers sent me in for retakes.

Another quirk: I often pronounced words incorrectly. Tulips were lutips, daffodils were laughodils, apricots were (still are) acripots. Maybe something was wrong with my brain. Or maybe I just liked the words better that way.

One day, Sister Bea asked my parents to come to her office in the parish convent. Real Dad and Stepmom sat at one end of a long sofa. I hugged the other end. Sister sat at her desk. She talked about my lousy study habits. "She's a smart girl, but she spends too much time writing notes to her friends."

I said I wasn't writing notes. At least not very many.

Sister Bea looked over her glasses, stood, picked a shoebox up off her desk. She walked over to me, took the lid off the box and dumped a couple hundred folded paper triangles over my head.

The only thing I remember between being dumped on and being grounded for the rest of the semester is hearing Sister Beatrix say, "She's obviously going to be a writer."

THE BELL AT OUR LADY

Our Lady Academy, Manteno, IL
Second Half of Sophomore Year

The church bell at Our Lady Academy tolled when anyone in the little town died. We knew what the ringing meant and would stop what we were doing to count the tolls.

Was it a man or a woman? Adult or child?

One afternoon in class the sister stopped lessons so we could say special prayers for a boy in town who was desperately ill. I don't think we knew the cause, but we did know that he was six years old. A kid. He could be our little brother. We wondered if he would ever get better. Now it seemed that he would not.

When the bell started tolling, we held our breaths, hoping to hear the code that meant an elderly person had died. Someone who was ready for it, perhaps in a family that was also ready. If it was a woman the bell would toll three times and rest, toll and rest, two sets of three.

1-2-3, 1-2-3.

If it was a man, we would hear three sets of three.

1-2-3, 1-2-3, 1-2-3.

Then, after a longer pause, a new count would begin. One toll for each year of the person's life. We were in the classroom, hardly breathing.

Three sets of three. A male. A long pause. Then the age ...

One.

Two.

Three.

Four.

Five.

Six.

We waited for the Seventh. Seven tolls would mean the boy – our boy, by now – might make it through this day. But the seventh toll did not come.

THE MOUND AT SINSINAWA

St. Clara Academy, Sinsinawa, WI

Junior and Senior Years

In 1957, home to approximately 500 nuns and 97 girls. My room was in "Old Stone," the original edifice built in the 1840s, behind the tree on the right.

No, I wasn't a bad girl. A little outgoing, maybe, but not delinquent. And neither was anyone else in my class. We were, for the most part, girls whose parents wanted them to get a good education. Some very wealthy. Some poor but promising. Some from countries in political strife whose families were able to send them to safety. Some whose moms and aunts and even grandmothers attended St. Clara. A few whose parents were deceased or divorced. And a batch in every class – six in ours – who wanted to be nuns.

Except for an occasional flash in the pan, I didn't want to be a nun. I was barely even Catholic. I got to the Mound because my dad and a priest from our home parish were drinking buddies. The priest knew about St. Clara's. It was an excellent school, he said. The nuns had high standards. They were into education, not punishment. Classes were small. Girls could have private rooms. All my dad had to do was take me there. See if the sisters thought I'd fit in.

Sister Marie Peter met us at the door. She led us up steep wooden steps and down the hall to her office – a narrow room with a tall window at the far end, a desk, and a long table where she invited us to sit. I sat holding my stomach while she and Dad discussed the school – the curriculum, sciences, philosophy, music, the yearly schedule, uniforms, fees. Finally, Sister turned to me. Did I think I'd be happy at St. Clara? Yes, I said, and nearly swallowed my tongue.

What was there to be happy about? Life in a convent boarding school with 97 girls, 500 nuns and the nearest boy eight miles away in Dubuque? Dad would be happy with this. Not me.

Suddenly angels started singing. "Novices," said Sister. "The chapel is just up the stairs." Such lovely voices. Dad stared out the long window like he had gone to some other place. He was hooked. And I was screwed.

It turned out to be two of the best years of my life.

We wore navy blue suits and beanies on weekdays. Chapel veils on Sundays. Ate our meals in the refectory. Homemade everything, mostly from the convent gardens. A favorite: homemade bread with butter, ketchup, and a spoonful of sugar.

My room was a hangout. Girls draped over chairs and the bed, listening and sometimes dancing to Chuck Berry (Roll Over Beethoven), Elvis Presley (Heartbreak Hotel), and Dave Brubeck (Take Five). We drank lukewarm Coke and thought up activities that were on the line between an "A" (acceptable) and a "B" in conduct.

Dad thought I was doing pretty well getting Bs. He didn't realize As were expected. You got Bs for things like smoking behind Mary's shrines. (Not me.) Or taping straws end to end to suck altar wine out of the keg in the basement. (Yes, me.)

Me, sitting on the long steps up to one of Mary's shrines, Lourdes or Fatima, I don't remember which or why I was sitting there.

Did we take our schoolwork seriously? Of course we did. I was a little less serious than some, but still good enough to write, in rhyme, a ridiculous play starring an Ugly Duckling who wailed her loneliness loud enough to rock the auditorium
and all the nuns in it.

One of the things I didn't realize at the time was how much energy Sister Marie Peter put into me. There were times when the situation at home nearly wiped me out. Promised visits didn't happen. My baby brother died. There wasn't room for me at home during the funeral.

I wasn't sure there was a God.

Sister Peter would call me down to her office to talk – as in conversation, not preaching – about religion, life, the light and dark threads in the tapestry. She agreed that my fourth-grade teacher was wrong about my parents going to hell and taking me with them. But even in my sweetest moments she wouldn't agree that I should be a nun. She thought I'd make a better mother.

During the Hungarian Student Revolt in 1956, thousands were killed and injured as they protested the USSR's domination of Hungary. We were upset that the United States did not support the students as promised. Our Sisters – nearly all of whom had master's degrees and had lived somewhere else in the world, re-organized classes to cover the history, the culture, the potentials, the probabilities. Rather than force feeding their opinions, they opened doors for us. They let us think. They let us talk.

The part-priest, part-architect founder of St. Clara, Father Samuel Mazzuchelli, would have been pleased. He taught women Rhetoric, Philosophy, Astronomy, Physiology, Chemistry, Geology, Geometry, Plane Trigonometry, Latin and French – in 1846! There's a tag line on an early brochure for St. Clara, "... the highest achievement of a female student is not a marvel of embroidery. Sewing lessons are fine. But we can do more."

THE MARTIN HOUSE

The kitchen window is tall and wide. Standing near it, I can see down the hill to the flat surface of Mirror Lake. Between the window and the water there's a tall pole with a Martin house on top. The house is white, with pillars and porches that remind me of the Grand Hotel on Mackinac Island. Dad built this Martin house and made another like it for one of my sisters. It doesn't seem outlandish to ask if he'd make one for me. But apparently it is. To my stepmother, at least.

"What makes you think your father would do that for you?"

My stomach knots. Once again, I have mismeasured the moment.

My stepmother's name was Jane. She came into the picture one afternoon when I was sitting on one of the spinny stools at the drug store near Dad's new apartment at the Jackson Hotel. He was sitting at one end of the counter. Jane was at the other. I was between them, feeling the heat fly from one to the other. I wonder now if I knew before they did that something was going on, something more than it was with other women he knew. He didn't know this one. She was pretty. Not as pretty as Mom, of course, but younger, glancing his way, smiling at me.

Over the next several years Jane became more and more a part of Dad's life – and mine. When Mom said she didn't have enough money to buy me an Easter hat, Dad showed up with a whole new outfit – a dress, a houndstooth coat with a matching shoulder cape, a French beret, white socks, and patent leather shoes. Even I could tell he wasn't alone when he picked that out. Mom was so upset she snatched the hat off my head and threw it on the sidewalk.

Mom called Jane The Diz. When I came home after a day or a week with Dad, Mom would ask, "Was The Diz there with you?"

I tried not to answer.

Dad and Jane spent a lot of time in bars. Nice ones, nightclub-like. He was proud that she could keep up with him, drink for drink. Mom could not. She didn't drink or smoke.

When the divorce was final, Dad married Jane. Mom married Steve, a Croatian who didn't like the way I chewed food. Life turned into a new tug of war. Who would pay for the dentist? Why was I wearing that ridiculous dress?

Jane's thing was to buy me clothes. Mom got upset when I wore them. Jane got my hair cut.

Mom cried at the loss of my braids.

I felt like a bird flitting back and forth looking for the right place to land. Jane had her first baby when I was eleven, and another one every two years after that.

My little sisters: Lynn, Carol, Mary, and Nancy.

I adored the kids, was always, always happy to take care of them. Jane said she never worried about them while they were with me.

That made me feel good.

When Dad got custody of me and I was finally coming to live with them, Jane went shopping. She bought a tanker jacket. Hammer pants. White socks thin enough to roll down inside the heels of my shoes. Everything she thought I'd need to fit in with my new life. When she saw that the clothes were wrong for the suburb we lived in, she went shopping again. The new sweaters and wool crew socks made me feel like she cared. I think she did.

The honeymoon lasted until Halloween Eve. I was babysitting when the gremlins rang the bell for trick or treat, and I realized we had no candy. No pennies I could find. The only things that seemed semi-reasonable were the fudgesicles in the basement freezer. Melting wasn't an issue; the kids devoured them immediately. Nothing was an issue until Jane got home. She hit the ceiling. What the hell was I thinking? How stupid could I be? You don't give kids fudgesicles for Halloween!

What should I give them? Martinis?

I didn't actually say that. But I'm sure I thought it.

She was often nice. And just when I got used to it, she got not-nice. One snowy day, she said I could invite friends over to try out my new toboggin. She drove us to the hill at Currie Park. Picked us up. Fed us spaghetti. It was a great day until Dad got home. Suddenly, it was a terrible day. The kids were loud. They stayed too long. They ate too much. She'd never, ever do that again.

I couldn't seem to get ahead of things. Another time, we were on a trip to Ontario with a neighbor couple and their son. The first day was fine until after dinner when the boy and I were told to stay in the cabin while the parents hung out in the lodge. Our cabin was seriously cold. The boy shivered and cried until I built a nice little fire in the Ben Franklin. All was well until Jane saw what I'd done and turned it into a major scene. How dare I? I could have burned the place down.

You'd have thought I set out to fry the boy.

A sad thing about these scenes was how quickly things turned from pleasant to ugly. We might be having guests for dinner, and Jane would prepare a fabulous meal – she was a fine cook. And before long she'd be scolding me, telling our guests how evil I was to have done this or that. Sometimes Dad would say, "Jane, take it easy." But he didn't put much oompf in it. The guests would leave. One night when Jane's mother defended me, Jane slapped her, in the face, hard. Her mother came to my room, said I should go live with my mother. "If you don't get out of here, Jane's going to kill you." I didn't know if she meant kill me physically or kill me emotionally. I tried extra hard to keep my head down. That's what Dad said I should do. "Keep your head down when she gets that way."

It wasn't like she beat me. Or locked me in the closet for days. I suspect people who didn't see the every-day of things thought we were doing fine.

Late in the summer between my Freshman and Sophomore years, Jane went to visit her relatives in Minneapolis. The living and dining room were to be painted while she was gone, and I was to have the house clean by the time she returned. The painters took longer than expected, and she came home earlier than anticipated. I was just getting started with the cleaning when she came in the door – a whirlwind of bitter accusations. What was the matter with me? Why wasn't everything clean like it was supposed to be? She flew up and down the stairs like a banshee, grabbed my suitcase, threw my things into it, shoved me out the front door. I was not to come back. Did I hear her? She meant it. I was good for nothing. She didn't know why my father let me come to live with them in the first place. It was certainly not that he wanted me.

The lady next door called me from where I was standing at the curb and took me into her house. She would have kept me with her, but that would have been too close to Jane for either one of us. I called a cab and went to see Father Albers, a priest who'd been kind to me at school and who I hoped would have some ideas. He got me to call an aunt who let me stay at her house. After a month or so, Dad arranged for me to stay with a friend of his until I went off to boarding school.

At our first home break, I took the train from Manteno, Illinois to Milwaukee and arrived not knowing where I was going to stay. Jane met me. Dad stood in the background, near enough to hear but not be part of the conversation. Jane was teary. She said she wanted me to come home. She was sorry. Dad was not living at home and would not come back unless, and until, I was there. Would I, please?

I can't say I was confident, but I said yes anyway. She took me straight to Smartwear and started buying. This skirt. That sweater. The other one, too. Blouses. Underwear. Jackets. Coats. The pile on the counter got taller and taller. I stood there, staring. The salesclerks did the same. It would have been funny, if the air hadn't been sizzling with tension.

The tab was $400. The year was 1954. You could buy a helluva lot of clothes for $400 in 1954.

Where was Dad in all this? He and I had a relationship on the side. He came to visit at school and when he saw that I was gaining weight on the noodle diet (all the way up to 110), he said, "Something is wrong here," and started shopping for a nicer boarding school.

I spent the summer in Cleveland with my mom and in fall, transferred to Saint Clara Academy – a school I learned to love... after a teen-age while.

In April, my infant brother died from a congenital heart problem. He was the only boy Dad and Jane had. I took the train home from school to Milwaukee, again not knowing where I'd be staying. A friend of Dad's met me at the station. There wasn't room for me at home. I hurt, but I knew Dad and Jane were hurting more. Uncle Warren flew in from Kansas and stood with me through the funeral. The sight of that tiny casket will never leave my brain.

For the last two years of high school, I spent vacations with my mom, or Gram, or the families of friends. I was lucky to always have someone to grab me when I might fall.

Mom and my stepdad came to my graduation. Dad and Jane did not.

We went up and down like that through all the years. When Jane was in rehab, Dad would call me to come take care of the girls.

During rough times he would call to talk, or we'd meet for lunch. When I asked him why he didn't stand up for me he said he grew up without a dad, and I grew up half that way, he didn't want to do that to another batch of kids. He said he knew I could handle it.

Years and many ups and downs later, when he was heading toward his end, he called to say he'd changed his will. He and Jane had fought about their wills for years. He wanted things to come out even for me and the kids they had together. She didn't see any reason to include me. Now he was sorry, but he just couldn't carry the fight any longer. Whatever they had would go to Jane. She would distribute it fairly.

Did I laugh? Yes.

Aunts, uncles, friends, made their feelings known. When Dad told Aunt Claire and Uncle Marvin about the new will, they got up from the table, went out the door and to their attorney's office and changed their wills giving all to me. From then on, when Dad or Jane did something unpleasant, Aunt Claire would say, "Don't worry. You're going to come out ahead."

The last time I saw my dad was a few weeks before he died. He called, asking for us to have lunch. He couldn't drive, and he could barely walk, but he managed to sneak out of the house. What a silly, sad, thing that he had to sneak out of his own house. Then again, he helped to make it that way.

He rallied while we were at lunch, told stories like when he was the young man at the bar, and I was the little girl who adored him.

Back at his home, in the driveway, he held onto my car door and, I think, tried to say, "I love you." That might be my imagination. He took a playful swing at me and stumbled up the stairs to the kitchen door.

At Wehr Nature Center, where a friend and I often walk, there's a straw-colored field spreading out and around a tall pole that holds up a martin house. It has pillars and porches like the Grand Hotel. I think I need to book a room there. I'll pretend I'm a bird. A Martin, maybe. I'll search the rooms and find a home in that pretty house.

I'll love everybody in it, and they'll love me.

How do I count thee? Once upon a time, there were 8 semi-siblings - 5 of them full blood, 2 halves, and 1 step. Two of the eldest and two of the youngest passed on, leaving 3 full blood and one half. That's four, all girls, all look a little alike, all refer to the group as "Sisters." The bond they formed when they were young still holds. They – make that *We* – stand together at weddings and funerals. We look at pictures of ourselves and think, Isn't that interesting? Which one is the half?

THINGS I WISH I HADN'T DONE

Preferred my dad, and sometimes even my stepmother, over my mom. She didn't deserve that, and neither did they.

Given away my first Raleigh racer.

Daydreamed through arithmetic.

Waited so long for boys to show up. And left so many others waiting.

Let my lawyer friends nominate me for Miss D.C.

Young Republican when I didn't know a DEM from a GOP.

Married Husband #1 without going all the way.

Married Husband #2 before I knew he was doing quite a lot of that.

Let #2 talk me out of adoption.

Waited 10 years to marry #3.

HUSBAND NUMBER ONE

When I met him, he had charm, good looks, a steady job. We had the same friends, watched the same games. He'd had surgery for spina bifida and wore braces on his legs, but that didn't stop him. He played baseball (with a buddy running the bases. His mother didn't approve of us marrying, but neither did my dad, so that was even. He was 20, I was 18 and of all dumb things, a virgin. That was a thing in the 1950s.

The morning of the wedding, I thought about running away. Brides often panic, I knew. But what do you do with the three hundred guests who were coming? Way more than I had expected.

My dad showed up at the church even though he said he wouldn't. He repeated that I was too young to get married. There was a car outside. Keys in the glove compartment. I could take it and head on down the road.

Real Dad left by a side door and Stepdad walked me down the aisle. My mom – freshly out of the hospital and short on oxygen, sat in the front pew, wheezing. We didn't know why guests kept chuckling until later when we found out that every time the maid of honor knelt down, her hoop skirt flew up in back, showing her garter belt and the world's prettiest legs. People remembered that for a long time.

We ran out of food at the reception, but I don't know that anyone noticed. The young ones drank. The older ones danced. My uncles – the fun ones on my mom's side – put on a mock wedding with a tipsy minister and a mop-wigged bride whose father chased the groom around with a squirt gun.

Around midnight the groom and I left, dragging tin cans and old shoes behind his beat-up Mercury. "Just Married." First stop, a hotel in Oshkosh. Number One neglected to make a reservation. The only room they had left was a little gray box with a three-quarter bed. It didn't matter. I was ready.

The wedding night was a bust of spectacular proportions. It turned out the groom was impotent – completely, physically, permanently, impotent. And as if that wasn't enough, he was also incontinent. I woke up in a wet bed. I didn't know the words for it at the time – didn't know what to do or what to say. Apparently, neither did he.

I should have run away that night, in the dark, found my dad and admitted I was wrong. But I didn't. I entered a four-and-a-half-year illusion in which I pretended everything was fine.

At Christmas, we had dinner at his grandparents' home. The long table was laden with homemade ravioli and garlic bread, a huge ham, tomatoes and green beans drizzled with olive oil. Plates were passed as people chatted about food and family. His grandmother said something about babies and stared straight at him. He said, "Well, it was supposed to be a surprise, but we think Judy's pregnant."

He looked as if he meant it.

A few months later he quit his job and said he could not find another. No one was hiring men in braces. It was an insurance thing, he said.

I don't know where my brain was, not then, not later when life changed even more radically.

We were having dinner with friends. The couple started arguing and before long voices were raised, plates flying, car keys hidden. The husband smashed his wife into the kitchen wall, the garage door, the hood of their car. I tried to stop him, and Number One pulled me out of it.

On the ride home, we argued, and he hit me for the first time. But not the last.

It's hard to talk about the next two years. I wrote a magazine article about it years later, after an old classmate said no man would dare hit her, she'd see to that. I wondered what she'd do if her husband dragged her by the hair across the ball field at a community picnic and no one interrupted. I take that back, at the far end of the field, just before the parking lot, a girlfriend of mine yelled at Number One to stop, and I had hope until her husband told her to be quiet.

I have great sympathy for women who don't or can't get out of ugly situations. I was pretty strong, but I'd never before seen a man behave like that. Never felt such meanness. Never imagined how it would feel to get a fist in the face or be kicked around a kitchen floor. I had a job and friends and family I could turn to.

But I didn't.

In the cooler light of today, I can see the reasons why. Then, I couldn't see anything except the blood and pain and fear and shame.

Eventually, I did leave. And he did as he promised – he tracked me down and tried to kill me. For four days he tied, tortured, and choked me. When he thought I was dead (and so did I), he walked into the kitchen, put his head down on the table and cried. I don't know how I knew this, but I somehow saw him there, and I somehow stood up and walked to the kitchen doorway and said, "I'm still alive."

It should have ended there. But it didn't. For years he stalked, and I hid. Hiding sounds easy to people, but to do it you have to give up family and friends and your job and all the everyday things that are familiar to you. If you have kids, you live with unimaginable fear. Even without them, for forty years, until I was in my 60s, I never parked my car without wondering if he was near.

Then one day I went online and saw his obituary. I just sat and stared. In it, he seemed like a nice guy. Devoted to his mother. Missed by nieces and nephews. "Gone to play poker at the big table in the sky."

I tried to remember good things about him, about our time together. There had to be some good times. But I couldn't think of any. All I could remember was the way he looked when he was angry, the cold eyes, the tight jaw, the fast-fast movement of his arm and fist.

LEARNING THE HARD WAY

I'm holding my breath.

Shelia and I haven't talked since we were in high school. Now, thirty-five minutes into a phone call, Shelia is updating me on a former classmate. "She's single again. I heard that her husband beat her. I'd like to see any man try that with me."

"How could you stop him?"

"I just wouldn't put up with it, that's all."

"What if he beat you anyway?"

"I'd call the police."

"What if he smashes the phone?"

"I'd get out of there."

"With him blocking the door?"

Her next response blows me away. This intelligent, well-educated, single mother with a great career says, "Well, she should never have asked for it in the first place!"

I wish Shelia was the only one who thought that way. Unfortunately, many people, men and women, ask: What did she do? Why did she sign on to that jerk? The questions keep the focus on the victim. It's like asking the woman who's been raped what she wore, or why she didn't run faster.

I wish, like Shelia, I could believe it couldn't happen to me, that I am protected by my class, race, family background, education, or neighborhood. It would be nice to think battery was a part of some culture other than mine. But women of all ages and backgrounds are battered every day in cities, suburbs, farms, mansions, back alleys, and parking lots. I know. I was one of them.

The warning signs of potential batterers weren't well known in the 50s. Even if they had been, I'm not sure I would have interpreted the violent arguments I saw in my fiancé's family as a sign he'd hurt me. He didn't for the first two years we were married. Then one night, he did.

What went on is no news to people who work with batterers. They know that bullies blame the women they beat, and that the women do what all hostages do. They get confused, wondering what they did to deserve this. Families and friends, if the women dare to talk to them at all, often add to the confusion by giving them sympathy on one level and sad advice on another.

They say, "Just do what he wants." (It's impossible to do what he wants. Batterers change what they want ten seconds before the next beating.)

They say, "It takes two to tango." (Not when one is bigger and meaner than the other.)

They say, "Couldn't you be a little sweeter?" (It's hard to be sweet when you've been punched in the face.)

"Can't you two work it out? You looked happy last week." (Last week, I believed it would never happen again. This week it's worse than ever.)

"What did you do to deserve it?" (You have heard this so many times you think that maybe you do deserve it.)

"Well, you're still there, aren't you?" The implication is that you are either too weak-willed to leave – in which case you're "asking for trouble" – or you must be having fun.

As a rule, a woman stays because it is her home, or she must take care of her children, or he says he'll kill her if she leaves. It's pretty much never that she's having fun.

In an article I wrote for *Wisconsin Women Magazine*, I told how my husband trapped me in the house for four days, punching me, dragging me around by my hair, tying me to the bed while he bit and scratched. I got loose once and ran to some friends. When they left for a few minutes, he broke into their house and threatened me in front of their two little boys. "No," I begged, "not in front of the kids." He said, slow and deadly, "That's how I know you'll come with me." He grabbed my arm and pulled me down the stairs, reminding me that I wouldn't want the kids to see blood. Two days later, when I got out again, I went to the police to press charges. The sergeant said it might be more trouble than it's worth. My husband would be out on the street in no time.

When I went back for clothes the next day, my husband was waiting, hiding behind a door. The friend who went with me pried his hands off my neck. I was hysterical when the police arrived. My husband was calm. He told them I was a screaming bitch. The officer said, "I feel for you, Buddy."

Men have historically been allowed, even encouraged, to "keep their women in line."

The "rule of thumb" gave husbands permission to use a stick to beat their wives as long as the stick was no bigger around than their thumbs. "A wife, a dog, and a walnut tree, the more you beat them, the better they'll be."

I wrote about this, but I didn't talk about it for a long time, because I hated the way people looked at me. I was also afraid. My husband's threats seemed real, especially when I found out, after relocating, changing my name, and spending months in hiding, that he was still out looking for me.

Something in me snapped during that conversation with Shelia. I think I'll have plenty to say the next time anyone jokes about "keeping the little lady in line."

The first thing I'd do is give girls and boys this list of questions to consider.

- Has he ever hit you? Pushed you? Twisted your arm? One act of violence breaks the taboo.
- Has he ever hit a former girlfriend – no matter what he says she's done to "deserve it."
- Is he violent with other men?
- Is he violent with animals?
- Can he handle frustration, or does he get angry and clench his fists with the slightest provocation?
- Does he threaten to hurt you? Shake his fist at you or anyone else?

- Does he try to control the way you dress, whom you see, how you spend your money?
- Does he treat you as if you're helpless without him? Too much doting undermines your independence, keeps you under his control.
- Does he call you names?
- Does he try to cut you off from family and friends?
- Is he extremely jealous?
- Can he accept blame for problems, or is it aways someone else's fault?
- Will he discuss problems, or does every discussion turn into an argument?
- Is he happy for you when you have successes, or does he minimize your achievements?
- Is his family violent, overtly or through verbal abuse?
- Does he get violent when drinking, or use alcohol or drugs as an excuse for violent behavior?
- Does he change personality quickly, from charmer to bully and back to charmer again?
- Does he treat you like a sex object, or demean you either with infidelity or the refusal to have sex?
- Do you see signs that he feels powerless or ineffective in the world? Is his self-esteem so

low that power over you seems important to him?

I wish I'd had this list to give Shelia.

I wish I had read it for myself.

GIRL GONE WILD

The studio apartment near downtown Milwaukee felt safe when the door was locked. I folded the sofa bed every morning, put on my high heels and walked the block to the bus stop, where the wind whistled down Wisconsin Avenue and up my skirt. At work, I pretended I'd always been single. If I was a little goosey when someone came up behind me, I didn't say why. My goal was to stand tall, look carefree, not show my fear of the shadows.

I was 23 years old and had a lot of catching up to do.

My first single-person-love was an insurance agent I did not even bother trying to resist. All he had to do was snap his fingers and I was there, sometimes in embarrassing places – farmers' fields, back seats, bathroom floors. He tried like hell to get me pregnant. When that didn't work, he displeased me greatly by getting someone else pregnant.

While I was crying about that, I fell for my boss, who was older, debonair, and not the least bit interested in getting me pregnant. After a few months of fancy dinners and nights on the town, I got a call from my dad. He said to meet him at the Holiday House. He wanted to talk.

"You need to leave town."

"What?"

"Leave town. The man you're seeing has a wife and son."

I stared at my fork.

Dad said he was the last one to call the kettle black, but....

While I sat there, swirling, he had the waiter bring a phone to the table. "My daughter needs a car." By the time we left the restaurant I owned a used Oldsmobile. I packed it, and in no time was on the road to Washington D.C. to stay with my mom and Stepdad "until things got settled."

I wasn't in Washington long before I met the gorgeous, dark haired, blue eyed, law student who became the next love of my life – parties on The Hill, trips to New York, late night walks around the Tidal Basin, and rolls in the hay nearly everywhere – including on the long table in a Senate

Hearing Room. (I think of that every time I see the Senators on TV.) He walked me through my first college registration at American University.

After a couple years the boyfriend got cancer and I became his nurse – bedpans, dressings, everything it takes to care for someone who is desperately ill. When the law board said he could take his bar exams in the hospital, I quit my job and stayed with him day and night, reading law books, writing papers, and discussing cases, until he passed the boards.

The guy had a right to be self-centered while that was going on, but it got tiresome when he stayed that way after he was well, especially when he figured it was okay to have an affair with his secretary because, after all, look what he'd been through.

SUCH LOVELY TITS

In the eyes of the world, and sometimes my own eyes, I am the one who causes trouble. It's my place as a woman, the natural effect of breasts and eye-makeup and short skirts and sitting too long at the bar. But it began long ago. Before there was any reason for it. Before I had any idea why I felt guilty.

Two years old: In bed with my dad, taking an ordinary, cuddle-up-for-warmth nap. When I wake up, I see a tent in the sheet near his belly. I reach to see what that is, and he grabs my arm, pushes me away. He doesn't scold, doesn't really say anything and there's no reason for it. But I'm sure I've done something wrong.

Four: The big boy next door pushes me against a retaining wall, traps me between his legs. He unzips his pants. Wants me to touch it. I don't like the looks or the smell of it. I push him over backwards and run away.

Six: I'm in the basement trying to balance the new two-wheeler I got for Christmas. I'm alone. Mom and my sister are gone. No one is in the upstairs flat where we live, and the people who live downstairs are gone, too. The basement is colder than usual, but I don't care. I'm focused on the bike, happy to stay upright for four or five feet before I topple over. I hear a noise behind me, a shuffling on the cement. It's the man who lives downstairs. He shoves my bike out of the way, grabs me, drags me to a shabby chair in the storage bin and makes me sit on his lap. I punch and kick free, and after that, try to stay away from him. But one day while his wife is gone, he lures me into their apartment. He lays down on the couch and pulls me on top of him, straddled, fighting to get loose. He smiles. Says, "You like this, don't you?" I don't know why I don't tell anyone.

Seven: The bad boy in the neighborhood chases me with a 2x4, hits me on the head. He's hurt other girls, too, so we decide to get even. We pull him into the juniper bushes and stuff prickers down his pants. Because of this, I'm pretty sure I'll go to hell.

Twelve: My friend's uncle sits next to me on the couch, watching TV. When the others leave the room, he puts his arm around my shoulder and slides his hand down onto my chest. I bite his arm.

Fourteen: My big sister's husband kisses me. I don't stop him, so I know for sure it's my fault.

Fifteen: My girlfriends and I go downtown to walk the Avenue and pick up boys. A car stops. Three boys, kinda cute. I get the driver. He parks. I pull away. He slips a church-key out of his pocket and says, "You know what I could do to your face with this?" He stares at me for a long minute, pushes the car door open and says, "Get the hell out of here."

Seventeen: I smart-off to a boyfriend that I'm too quick, too strong, to be raped. He pushes me down on the car seat and gets on top of me, forces my legs apart. Says, "Don't be so goddamned stupid."

Eighteen: I get a job as a hospital nurse aide. A resident does my employment physical in an examining room. Alone. He has me take off my blouse, lie down, put my arms up over my head. He checks for breast lumps – for what seems like forever. I'm afraid to move. Afraid of him. Afraid I won't get the job.

Twenty-two: My soon to be ex-husband says if he can't have me, no one will. He ties me to the bed, bites, punches, rips with his fingers. He may be impotent, but he knows how to kill. My divorce attorney knows I can't pay. I don't know whether it's his fault or mine that we end up in a hotel room, but I don't want to be there. He undresses and heads my way, so excited that it's all over before he gets there.

Twenty-four: The pediatric neurologist I work for has a little girl sitting on the examining table. I see them through the open doorway. He tells her mom he needs to be alone with the girl, that Mom should leave the room and close the door behind her. The little girl looks at me with pleading eyes. I think it's normal doctor-fright until years later, when I find out what he's done to other little girls.

Twenty-five: My boss gets up from his desk, walks over to me and grabs my breast. I jerk away. He says I asked for it, walking around with such lovely tits.

So that's it. That's the problem. Lovely tits.

HUSBAND NUMBER TWO

Number Two and I met in 1968, when I was studying nursing at the University of Maryland during the day and working the night shift at Suburban Hospital. He was a Navy Corpsman stationed at Bethesda Naval Hospital, also working the night shift at Suburban. In the middle of one night, this gorgeous guy responded to a Code Blue, took over as if he was a doctor, and saved the patient's life. Before he left the room he paused and looked at me with deep brown eyes that wouldn't let go.

Six weeks later, I walked down the aisle at Bethesda Naval Hospital, my brain screaming, "What the hell am I doing?" I was about to yell, No! when I opened my mouth and said, Yes.

We were married 15 years – twelve good ones and three struggling to get "good" back again. Our first Christmas, we trimmed the tree with blue lights and twelve boxes of tinsel, hung one strand at a time. Tinsel was out of fashion by 1968, but the tree looked stunning in our little apartment. A box under the tree also looked stunning – silver paper, a huge red bow – and in it, the most ridiculously wonderful gift I ever got in my life. A white ostrich feather coat. The coat was splendid. The clerk at Saks thought I was crazy returning it, but have you ever tried to sit down in a coat made of ostrich feathers?

I soon learned how to iron his bell bottoms, also how to cook Texas chili, and that okra wasn't something you bought one of. "What do you mean, you bought an okra?" Number Two was an early bloomer – an actor on Houston's Alley Theater stage while he was still in high school, and one of the youngest stockbrokers in Texas when he turned 21. When his draft number came up, he joined the Navy medical corp. When he was about to be shipped to Vietnam, his doctor-boss got him assigned to the tower at Bethesda. There he cared for old officers who made calls on their IV bottles, and friends of his who came home with torn up limbs and faces.

He kept his night job at Suburban Hospital. I kept mine, too, until Chemistry and exhaustion blew me out of the student tubes. I took a job as a Girl Friday Do-Everything at a small financial firm. I was the office star for the first few years, until my boss hired my husband, made me train him, gave him a fancy title, and paid him twice what I was getting.

All in all, we had a solid marriage that included travels, new homes, a foster son, and his rise to VP of a global financial firm. It was a two-person career in which I was the second person. He sent flowers weekly, no matter where he was. One calendar quarter we were together for only four weekends, one each in New York, Tampa, Chicago, and San Francisco.

I should have known that couldn't last. One night he woke me up at 2 AM to say he was in love with someone else. He expected me to say, "Get out right now," but I didn't. It took us another three years to detach.

We said our last goodbye in Hawaii, where he had promised to take me one day. He got a phone call while we were there. I could tell by the look on his face, or maybe his breathing, that we were over.

DUANE

This is Duane, the foster son who delighted our days for a year in the early 1970s. He was a sad little boy when he came to live with us. He'd just turned five and was very angry, especially with his mom for drinking too much and leaving her three little boys alone. Husband Number Two and I did what we could to help him love his mom and still feel safe in our home.

Adoption was in the plan from the beginning – something the agency rarely did but thought was likely in this case.

When I think of Duane – which is often – I wonder if he remembers being with us. The trips we took. The people he met. The clothes he fell in love with. All things that were unlikely to have been part of his other life. He went from sad to happy in our house. From too quiet to noisy. From poor in school to pretty good. From fearful to confident.

He wet his pants for a week when he first came. I thought it was due to trauma until I noticed how keen he was on changing into his new clothes. All I had to say was, "I'll wash those things and you can have them back in a jiffy." He quit wetting.

I remember him at the Kennedy Memorial in Arlington Cemetery, standing up straight in front of my dad, saluting the old man who always wished he'd had a son. There were more emotions in that moment than I'll ever forget.

I remember the day he called me Mom. He stumbled over the word, "M-a-a-mom." I said, "How about Mama Judy?" That was fine.

At the end of the year his real mom came back. She and his dad, who had always been in the shadows, wanted to gather their boys together again. The law was thin, not in our favor. We didn't fight hard. Perhaps we should have. But the duel would have gone on forever and his visitations had him ready to "go home." Duane's memories changed. His mom never left. His dad was going to buy him a motorcycle.

We made plans to leave on a horseback trip minutes after Duane stuffed his favorite shirts into his duffel and hugged us goodbye. Packing for the trip kept us busy, kept me from sitting on the floor crying my eyes out.

Now and then I try to find him. But no. I never have.

MY TURN ON THE CROSS

Gram's voice is not the lullaby it was when I was little and hid around corners just to hear her call again. Now she sounds all gruff and scoldy. "Well," she says, "What are you going to do about it?"

I tighten my grip on the phone. "Do about what?"

"Your name. Are you going to change it?"

I'm newly separated from my husband, touchy, teary, not at all on her wavelength. "Why do you need to know?"

"Your gravestone. I need to know what to put on your gravestone."

The grave is important to Gram. She saved a space for me, next to hers in a beautiful little cemetery on a hill that slopes into Summit Lake. Pine trees, white birches, picture perfect. But it's the last thing on my mind right now. “Gram, I'm not dying.”

“Doesn’t matter. I want your stone taken care of before someone else gets bright ideas."

“What do you mean, bright ideas?” That was too snotty. It's the marriage. The loss of it. I don’t really want to let go. "Judith Weyenberg Bridges," I say. "First, maiden, married. Whatever happens, that will work."

She sighs hard enough to hurt the phone. Hangs up.

I forget about this for weeks, until my husband, newly returned to our home and in his office paying bills, says, "What the hell is this?"

I look over his shoulder. 'This' is the bill for my gravestone.

I call Gram. She put his name on the account. "If the man is back in the house, he can damned well pay the bill.”

He pays. Life goes on. We move with his company, from Virginia to Chicago to San Francisco, where we finally, really, split up. I move back to Milwaukee, alone. Gram lives 200 miles north. At last, I get to see more of her.

One sunny day we visit the graves. I carry her bag of last year's plastic flowers. Tulips for her mom. Sunflowers for her dad. Roses for Gram, even though she's still alive. Violets for two of her babies. And then mine.

"Uh, Gram?"

"What?"

"The year, 19-something. I don't plan on dying that soon." She waves me off. "You can get someone to fix it."

I stick the daffodils in the ground in front of my stone and imagine relatives I rarely see working their way down the line, past Great-Grandma, Great-Grandpa, Gram, the babies. They come to mine, see the plastic daffodils, say, "Gee. I didn't know Judy died. Did you know Judy died?"

A new job forces me to slow down on visits to Gram. I send cards every few days. In one, I say how nice it is to have a smart, funny, feisty grandmother like her. She calls. The phone is almost burning. "Feetzee! How dare you call me Feetzee! That's a terrible thing to say!"

I don't know what she thinks feisty means, but it's bad enough that she no longer wants me buried near her. I should come get my gravestone.

"Gram, I can't just get my gravestone. "

"You best see to it!"

I've seen her like this before, when she's had it with one of her sisters, a daughter-in-law, or the lady across the hall. She hangs the offender on the cross for a year or so, until the next sinner comes along. But until this feetzee thing, it never happened to me. I stayed under the radar and honestly got to thinking I was special. Maybe she loved me best after all.

She keeps calling, asking when I'm going to retrieve the stone. She says there is space for it at Holy Cross Cemetery in Milwaukee. She knows, she checked on it. All I have to do is pick it up and take it there.

One day, she leaves a message. "It's all settled. Allied Van Lines will pick up the stone and deliver it to your apartment."

I call my dad. He tries to stay out of these things, but I beg. "Please, find a way to calm her down. She's going to ship that thing down here and what am I going to do with it?"

He laughs. Suggests I carry it in the trunk of my car. "You never know when you might need it."

"Dad!"

"She'll get over it."

She did, eventually, forgive my transgression and pass the cross on to a cousin who also didn't deserve it.

Gram is gone now, and despite our time of tension, I miss her terribly. Every summer I drive up to Summit Lake with a bag full of plastic tulips and daffodils and walk down the row, planting them in the ground on the family graves.

Including Gram's.

Including mine.

WITH NO LOVE IN IT

The face was as handsome as I remembered. Skin slightly weathered. Blue eyes. A little gray in the brows. Lips that made me want to touch them. And below the face, a body I knew would fit perfectly to mine.

He didn't speak. Neither did I.

I held out my hand. He took it and followed me to the bedroom. Without words, we slid out of our clothes and made love. All evening. Tender, curious, fulfilling love. As if we knew exactly where to go, what to touch. As if there was no need to think about a beginning, or an end.

There was no real beginning. Weeks earlier we sat at separate tables at Beans and Barley eating the day's special squash soup and baguettes cut on the bias. We were each blowing steam off the soup when he caught my eye, and I caught his and neither of us looked away. We ate and left without speaking. He walked south. I walked north to my apartment, all the way thinking, "That man is going to find me." I didn't know how. I just knew he would.

He called a few weeks later. I did not ask how he found me. I said hello, hesitated a moment, and gave him my address. I was surprised at myself, but not upset. All of my upset was being used by another man – the one who capped our 15th anniversary with the news that he'd met (and slept with) the perfect woman. Our life together was over.

All I wanted was the heat of an affair with no love in it. Nothing to lose. The new guy, Charles, was a professor at the university. He said his last love was a tall blonde dancer who took him to New York and introduced him to Twyla Tharp. That romance was over. He had a screenplay he hoped to sell to Hollywood. He wasn't looking for love any more than I was.

I forgot his last name almost as soon as I heard it.

But the heat continued. One night I met him at the door in cowboy boots, jeans, and a silk blouse. After he took care of that, I showered and slipped into a black negligee. The next morning, I put on a terry bathrobe and cracked eggs for breakfast. He ran his fingers around the collar of the robe and the eggs were forgotten.

We never went to his apartment. Always mine, and I was quite content with that. I had my bed. My towels. My call on what time he came over. I was the one in control. If I didn't love him, he couldn't hurt me.

It wasn't long before I noticed we didn't get on as well standing up as we did lying down. He dressed oddly, for one thing. One night he showed up in a black watch plaid cape so long it swirled around his ankles. He thought it was quite charming, I thought he looked like a re-fried horror writer.

But I slept with him anyway.

He suggested a trip to L.A. He had a chance to meet a producer he hoped would be interested in his screenplay. I would love it. We took my car because it had a working air conditioner. In Omaha, we stopped for lunch with an old, dear friend of mine who kept staring at Charles like he was from another planet. Charles ignored my friend. He was busy scolding the bus boy for pushing a carpet sweeper around and under vacant tables while we were still eating. I admit the sweep was annoying, but who scolds a bus boy?

In Denver, we stopped for gas and for the second time he hung back while I paid the bill.

Somewhere around Lake Mead we stopped at a roadside motel. Charles got his heat up. I was not interested. He made a little speech about sex being the only thing we had going for us and where did I get off withholding.

In L.A. we carried our suitcases into a spare room attached to his friend's garage – a greasy spot with a lumpy bed that almost made me cry for home.

The first night he went off to a party with film people and came back very late, a little high, and ready for action.

He didn't get any.

All the next day I waivered from chastising myself for getting into this spot and calculating how to get out of it. His rants escalated from "Withholding" to "Withholding Bitch!" He held the cards. He was bigger than me and knew the area. Worse, because he drove the car last, he had the keys.

The day, the evening, the beginning of the night, passed in unbearable tension. It got worse after he fished a flask out of his duffel. No, I didn't want a drink. No, I didn't think it would be nice to warm me up, to make me more loving.

Around midnight he fell asleep in his clothes, deep into a hard-snoring pattern – In. Out. In. Again. As long as I heard the sound, I felt somewhat safe. I took the phone in the bathroom, buried my face in a wad of towels, and called my sister in Milwaukee: "If you don't hear from me by morning, send in the cavalry." Then, with my heart beating like crazy, I slid my fingers into Charles' pants pocket to get the keys, and quietly, oh so quietly, closed the door behind me.

I almost panicked when I got near the car. What if he heard me? What if he gets here before I can lock the door, before I can get too far away for him to bang on the car, break the window?

I knew what he'd say. Not say, yell. That I'd led him down the road to perdition and cut him off, high and dry. Left him without a car.

My nerves settled as I drove north on U.S.1, Sierra Madres on my right, Pacific beaches on my left, L.A. fading behind me.

HUSBAND NUMBER THREE

The guy reaching for the bird house is my husband, Dave. He's replacing the old house that fell in the snow last year. It was pretty well done with. The base was soggy, and the Green Bay Packer G was ragged all along the edges. What was left of the little house didn't add up to a fit place for a wren or her babies.

We asked the woman who moved into the apartment next to us if she'd miss it if we threw it away. She said her husband had recently passed. Because he was a Packer fan, the house seemed like a welcome to her, as if a bit of him was still with her. This made Dave decide to repair it.

I don't know how he replaced the missing pieces. His works of art generally include tongue depressors and duct tape. I do know he took chips of the old paint to the magicians at the paint store and had them matched. Then he oh so carefully painted the Packer logo under the tiny round door. He set the house back a little further on the base so Mama Wren would have more room to stand while she shopped for a home for her babies. He knew the moms did that because he saw birdy- scratches on the old front porch.

Dave sees details like that. He's an actor and artist at heart. When dinner talk is about cranes making their first flight south, he wonders what would happen if the ultralight pilot quit leading and fell back in the V. Suddenly, he is the crane out in front of the flock, flapping his wings and yelling back at the plane to "Get off my tail!"

Dave sees lines and colors and shadows and what birds do that I don't see. When he draws an owl, or a flamingo, it looks like every feather is exactly where it's supposed to be, where it works best.

I didn't expect that Dave and I would make much of a couple when we first met. I was 43, in the middle of a divorce from the V.P. of an international firm. Dave was 31, single, delivering pizzas. We could be friends, I figured. We were both students at the University of Wisconsin-Milwaukee, active in a group called the Adult Student Alliance. The group earned a fair amount of respect on campus because we represented a new wave of non-traditional, aka "older," students. I spoke at events welcoming new students to college. Dave was the Grip, hauling mikes and handouts from here to wherever.

The first time we slipped over from "just friends" to something like a date, he asked me to join him for "dinner on the town." I dressed appropriately – nice dress, shoes, matching purse. I knew I was off-base when he showed up in faded jeans and a crumpled jacket.

Our first stop was in a park near the Milwaukee River where a particular tree sprouted edible somethings. Dave had a whole list of edible somethings and knew where to find them. We did indeed "have dinner on the town," eating leaves and weeds.

I had a list I wrote in a pocket spiral while I was sitting in the University library, not doing my homework. My list was what I wanted in a next husband: Someone who'd be there for me. Who was kind. Patient. Willing to play and be ridiculous. Not fussing about work all the time. Mostly, he'd be with me, permanently. We'd be a lively, devoted pair.

I tucked the list away and forgot about it.

Sometime later, I found the list and realized how prophetic it was. I perhaps had a lapse in not mentioning money, but everything else was there. He helped me move into my new house. He helped take care of Mom when she was ill. When we attended a cousin's wedding, he noticed that the bride's sister, who has Down's Syndrome, was standing on the dance floor all by herself, looking lonely. He excused himself from our table, walked up to her and asked if she'd like to dance.

Her smile was worth the world.

So was mine the night we were at a piano bar, and he sang Anthony Newley's "Who Can I Turn To." He looked directly at me the whole time. I didn't know where to put my eyes.

What a lovely voice. What a lovely man.

We hung out together for ten years, neither one of us too sure we could manage an actual wedding. The option that finally appealed to us was to fly to Scotland and get married in Gretna Green, a Marrying Town since the 1700s when English marriage law was strict and Scottish quick and easy. The town is filled with dioramas of English lovers racing across the border to the blacksmith's shop, wealthy fathers in hot pursuit hoping to stop their daughters from marrying the stable boy. The whole idea sounded like fun, especially since we didn't need to take witnesses with us.

We hand-made our announcements and took them with us, agreeing that we wouldn't mail them until after the deed was done. If we failed to get along the last day or two, we could just walk away. Couple of scaredy-cats, that's what we were.

When the day came, we checked in at what looked like a small-town Justice of the Peace. The clerk asked if our witnesses would be along soon.

"Uh, we understood there would be people here."

"Yes. Well, if you don't have anyone with you, you just go out on the street and ask people."

"What?"

"The Street. Just ask."

Ask perfect strangers? Neither of us was shy, but gee.

So, we sat on a park bench in front of the mini courthouse, eyeballing possible targets.

"How about that guy?"

"His boots are muddy."

"You think that's mud?"

"Yeah. Well. How about that couple?"

"Walking too fast. Must be busy."

Finally, two couples circled around the post box, busily stamping and mailing cards.

"Tourists! They might think this would be fun."

"Ask them."

"You ask them."

"I'm not going to ask them. You ask."

In the end, we went up to them together and stuttered our request. They were delighted. Off to the JP's little office we went. Just as we got near the door, one of the ladies tugged my arm.

"You are wearing your garter, aren't you?" Her accent was thick on gahrter. "You can't get married without a proper Tartan gahrter!" She caught my chagrined expression.

"That's okay, dearie. I have one!" She bounced down the street to their little red car and came back waving the garter. "Here 'tis! Here 'tis! You'll wear this!" She gave Dave instructions as he slipped the garter over my toes and up my leg. All four of our witnesses watched and laughed.

Our wedding announcement.

When the bloom is on the heather, we will wed, my love and I.

We were married in a short service in the JP's office. We didn't write special vows, just took what they had on hand – except that I checked in advance to be sure there was no mention of obedience. Dave agreed with that. He said he didn't want to obey me anyway.

When we got ready to leave, I realized I didn't know what to do with the garter. Was I supposed to give it back? Keep it? Neither sounded right. Our lovely witness caught my chagrin a second time. "Don't worry, dearie. You keep it. He'll buy me another." It turned out her husband had given her the gahrter as an anniversary gift. It was special to both of us.

We still keep in touch now and then. And yes, we still have the garter, in the photo album next to the one of us standing at the Blacksmith's anvil, Dave in a dusty top hat, me in a floppy veil. Perfect tourists doing what you're supposed to do in Gretna Green.

If ever I find that list of what I wanted in my next husband, I'll frame it. I'll hang it alongside the photo of Dave standing on a stepstool, inspecting the wren house for soundness and livability. He positioned it so it faces our neighbor's window, and the chairs where we sit watching for new mama wrens to arrive. When the time is right, they zip by with tiny sticks and bits of fluff and soon enough, food for their babies.

We watch them come and go and are grateful for another year together.

Dave and me on our 30th anniversary.

FOR THE LONG HAUL

I had to re-write the title for this. It started out as "Tips for the Bride and Groom." But as I wrote, I realized that was not enough. Promises to "Never go to bed angry," are sweet, but nearly impossible to keep. To get through the days when you are bored, stressed, crabby, and absolutely certain you married a self-centered nincompoop, you need stronger stuff. You need advice for the long haul.

With all best wishes to brides and grooms – and committed partners of any sort – long-haulers know they have pushed the edges of their marriage many times. They've sworn. Stormed. Thrown things. (I once threw a half-dozen raw eggs at my kitchen wall. Not my brightest moment.)

There are exceptions to this mayhem. My Aunt Claire swore she and Uncle Marvin had a perfect marriage, that they lived together for 55 years with "never a dust up." She said Uncle Marvin deserved the credit for their happy marriage because he just wouldn't argue.

I never married a man like that. All of my partners, husbands and otherwise, were perfectly capable of getting angry with me and kicking up a fuss. I helped them, of course. I'm not much like my Aunt Claire. In my 80- plus years of people-watching, I've seen very few pairings in which both parties were consistently calm and considerate. Life is not always full of lollipops and roses.

And yet, many of us spend long periods of, if not bliss, at least a few lollipops and roses. My dear one and I sway from biting our tongues to letting it rip and then to walking hand and hand. If we had not listened to the advice of other long haulers, we'd have killed this marriage long ago.

There is no perfect script, that is sure. But there are bits of wisdom. What helps? What hinders? I'm not asking the person who says they have a totally happy marriage. I want advice from people who are willing to say they screw up now and then and this is how they work their way back to each other.

BITS OF WISDOM

Say "I love you" at least once every day. Say it out loud, with no buts attached. It's not going to kill you. Chances are that beneath any irritation you feel at the moment, there is love. Dig it up.

Listen. Even if you've heard the story a million times. Try to be calm and process what you hear. Stay with it 'til the end.

Appreciate (out loud) any food your mate brings into the house or prepares for you. None of this, "If I don't complain, you know I like it." That was your grandfather's thing.

Clean up after yourself. No one enjoys picking up another person's dirty underwear.

Say good things about your partner's family – even if s/he doesn't. We get to make smart remarks about our own relatives, not theirs. The remarks bite in all the wrong places and stay bit.

Make note of things you'll never say, even if you're screaming angry. Cuts last forever. Even if it's true, do not say: "You're fat." "You're stupid." "Your mom's a bitch." "You're a failure." "It's that control thing of yours." Or "I've been faking it all along."

Respond nicely when s/he sends a make-up signal after an argument. Forego silent treatments. They're cruel and they say more about you than your mate. Give in quickly, even if it's to say, "I love you, but I need a little more time to settle down."

If you know something you do hurts the relationship – Flirting. Drinking. All-day golfing. Big spending. – Quit it. Nothing is worth the heartache of a divorce and if you keep it up, you're in for one.

If you're tempted to have an affair, don't. When I was in my 20s and seeing too much of my boss, my dad cornered me. "I've been there," he said, "I know this. You can't make yourself happy by hurting someone else."

This suggestion is unusual, but wise. If your mate has an affair and you think it's a one-time thing, consider forgiveness. If it looks like a habit, bail out slowly, deliberately. Do not panic. When you panic you do stupid stuff.

On the other hand, if your mate slaps you or pushes you up against a wall, get out as fast as you can. A slap is a match igniting a long burning fire.

If – when – you screw up, forgive yourself and your mate. You are both human, after all.

At the end of each day, comment on one nice thing your mate did that day. It wouldn't be a bad idea to write it down somewhere. Keep a list. Refer to it on days it's hard to think of something good.

And here's the capper. Kiss goodbye every time you leave. It doesn't have to be mushy, a peck on the cheek will do. This was my husband's idea. I've grown to love it. If something happens to him or to me, it will be our last sweet memory of the other.

MY LIFE IN PANTS

Soft pink bunting
Seersucker sun suit
Red wool snow suit, tailor made
Jodhpurs
Jeans
Pedal pushers
Hammer pants, with a bomber jacket and some guy's dog tags
Bell bottoms
Hip huggers, with halter tops, Ooo la la
Hot pants with purple boots, "Made for Walkin' Baby!"
Stove pipes
Katie Hepburn trousers
Stirrups
Tights
Straight legs
Capris
Rip Stop hikers, lots of pockets
Boot cut jeans
NYDJs
High rise
Black Pull Ons, heavy on the Lycra

THE FEZ

I didn't pay much attention when my stepdad got his fez. He was proud of being a Shriner and going to the Masonic Temple. I mostly teased him with dumb kid jokes like, "Hey, Dad! You going out with the Shiners? What'cha gonna shine? Ha. Ha."

He shrugged me off. What do kids know?

This kid wasn't even sure what to call him. He never said he wanted me to call him Dad, but Mom said I should. I went back and forth. "Dad" when people knew I was talking about this Dad. "Stepdad" when they might be confused. "Steve" when I thought it made me sound like a grownup. I'll call him "Dad" in this writing if that's okay with you.

Dad was a reserved man. A little cranky, actually. I didn't think he had much use for me, until he was quite old and had to start turning his life over to me, one slice at a time. At first, he needed help at the doctor's office. Then it was the checkbook. Then the car, the cooking, and eventually all the personal things he could no longer do for himself.

It was during those years that I finally got to know the immigrant kid, the little boy who came over “on the boat,” and grew up to head our household. As we sat in the doctor’s waiting room, or the hospital ER, he told stories about his youth, how he hated pushing that rickety cart around town collecting the scraps of wood his mom sold for food. Or, how his little brother John used to tag along, constantly chattering, whacking the side of the cart with a stick. One day John whacked too hard, and the cart tipped over on top of his big brother, pinning him beneath the pile of wood. John was terrified. His big brother was dead. John ran into the nearest tavern, flapping his arms, yelling at the top of his lungs, "I killed my brother! I killed my brother! And my ma's gonna kill me!"

According to Dad, the men from the tavern lifted the cart and hurried him to the nearest hospital, where he distinctly heard his mother promise that if he lived, he would never have to take that cart out on the street again. But when he was well enough, she sent him back out with the cart, an action he never understood, and never forgave.

In an era when few of the boys in his neighborhood finished high school, he was singled out for college. His mom put the kibosh on that. She needed him to keep working in the foundry to bring home the bacon. I wonder if he knew, even if she didn't, that the silica he breathed would get him in the end.

Dad was long out of the foundry, selling blind-made rugs and brooms, when he married my mom. His first wife, the mother of his son, died earlier that year. He would not have married so quickly if his old-world family hadn't pushed him to find another mother for his son.

My mom had the same thought – to have a father for her girls. She didn't tell me that at the time, probably because she knew I'd say I already had a dad. From the day Stepdad scowled at me in the rear view mirror and asked my mother if I was going to hug that goldfish bowl all the way to Grand Rapids, I decided not to like him, no matter what.

Truth is, he deserved better.

He made tomato soup and grilled cheese sandwiches when I was sick.

He held Mom's hand when the judge awarded custody of me to Real Dad.

He's the one in the photos taken at my high school graduation. He's the one walking me down the aisle. He's the one who let me come home when my life was a mess. He was there the day I got my bachelor's degree. And my masters.

We moved closer to each other the last few years of his life when we walked down the hard road together. He got mean for a while, tried to throw me down the stairs when I held him off of Mom. One time he grabbed the steering wheel when he didn't like the route I took home from the doctors' office. They diagnosed dementia. He got over the mean streak and came with me to Mom's memorial service, but he really didn't understand that she was gone. He looked dazed, kept his hand on his chest where he felt the worst of the cancer that was taking him away.

In order to move the hospital bed into his room, I had to wiggle his cedar chest into a far corner. When I emptied it to lighten the load, I found his birth certificate – a long scroll scripted in his native Croatian language. I found a photograph of him with his mother and sisters and brothers, all dressed in their Sunday best, standing stiffly in a photographer's fake living room.

I found the wedding ring he wore while married to his first wife, and a card commemorating her death.

There was a photo showing him costumed in the bright reds and blues of teenage folk dancers, and a Sunday magazine cover of him with his soccer team.

And I found the fez. It was wrapped in faded tissue, stored with his white leather Masonic apron and a copy of the Temple magazine, the *Almas Alibi*, August 1965. The hat was perfect – ornate gold lettering sewn onto stiff burgundy felt, Masonic symbols trimmed with sparkling red and gold, a rich black tassel dangling from the crown. It was easy to imagine Dad standing proudly, wearing this beautiful hat. At last, I understood him. Here was the immigrant kid who didn't speak English. The boy with the wood-cart, all grown up, wearing a fine hat, welcomed by a group of men he admired.

He died on Easter Sunday, 2001, at the age of 91. That morning, the hospice nurse left his meds with me and said to call when it was over. I held his hand for hours until I had to, just had to, go to the bathroom. I thought he might die in the minutes I was gone, but when I returned, he was still holding on. I took his hand and asked him a question that came out of nowhere.

"Do you need to know you were the best dad after all?"

This man who walked so proudly in his fez, who had not spoken for days and had not moved any more than to press his fingers softly into mine, nodded his head.

Yes.

And then he died.

THE PRICE OF INDEPENDENCE

Eva stands in the hosiery aisle at Woolworth's, shaking with anger. She glares at the baby-faced clerk like an eagle ready to attack. Suddenly the lines on her old face rearrange into a horrified look. There is a gushing sound. Her white summer shoes fill with the product of an irritated colon.

After a stunned silence, Eva lifts her shoulders, steps out of the reeking puddle and hurries from the store.

She lies to protect herself. "The doctor gave me the wrong cathartic." The lie is almost convincing.

"People like that uppity clerk think I'm feebleminded just because I'm old," she says to her younger companion. "Well, I have news for them. I'm not ready for the fox farm yet!" Eva shakes her head. There is a bruise on her cheekbone. Two weeks ago she collapsed on the sidewalk near the bank. Her story then was that a ruffian pushed her down. After spending a few hours in a hospital emergency room, she insisted on going home to her apartment. "If I'd have stayed at the hospital, they would have sent me to a nursing home. Once they get you, it's hard to get loose."

Eva is 92. She moved into her apartment in a northern Wisconsin town 12 years earlier, when her children started worrying about her living in the country without a phone, without running water. The apartment has oak floors, tall windows in the living room, and a dark wood archway between that and the dining room.

"It's nice here," she says. Not as nice as the big house she shared with her third husband, Bert. Not as nice as the white-washed log cabin in the country, with its wildflowers and berries. But as nice as you can get in town. The apartment is her private space. Her grandchildren can stay overnight. She can walk from there to the dime store, if the weather's good.

If the sidewalks are dry.

If she stops to rest along the way.

And, since the incident at the bank, if she can find someone to walk with her.

"You know, I used to walk miles in the woods. Every day. Alone. And pick berries. And garden. And do the canning. You never saw a healthier woman."

Eva sits in her favorite chair, the one with the peacock-patterned upholstery, and stares out the window. Sunlight catches in her silver braids, glances off the hairpins she uses to hold them in a tight circle around the top of her head.

Her eyes are a watery blue. Her nose is large. Her eyebrows are traced with dark pencil. When she crosses her legs, a fall of flamingo-colored lace can be seen under her dress. Suddenly she stops staring, spins around, animated. She has another story to tell.

This story is about Bert, the man Eva married when she was in her 60s. When Bert said she was too old to learn to drive, she got in his old Ford and turned the key. She put the car in gear and drove pell-mell around and around the house, with Bert running after, yelling at her to stop. She never told him she didn't know how to stop. She said she clipped off the back porch and the two young pine trees on purpose.

"Guess I showed him a thing or two, didn't I?"

Another story. She likes to tell this one. Her first husband came home from a logging trip and scared her and the kids. She shot him through the door and said if he was too dumb to say, "Honey, I'm home," he deserved to be shot."

The second husband was a "no-good." He drank and ran around with other women. She left him and waited a long time before marrying Bert. Bert's particular charm, according to Eva, was that "he was still alive at both ends." She likes to tell that story, too.

"I've had three husbands and I'll not have another," Eva says firmly. "All these old codgers want is someone to take care of them." One fellow, a bachelor, took her out to dinner every week for a year. He still visits, but he doesn't take her out to dinner anymore.

Father Donohue brings communion on Sundays. A county home-care provider checks on her every day. Meals on Wheels delivers soup in Styrofoam bowls.

"Sometimes I tell them not to bring the food. I can cook for myself."

But she leaves the burners on too long. The landlord worries. "I've had other tenants like her," he says. "Marvelous old women. But when their bodies give out, they get dangerous. She set the kitchen on fire a while ago. Didn't see the burner, I guess. I hate like hell to put her out."

When her daughter Claire visits, she pleads, "Mom, if you won't come live with us, would you at least give some thought to a nursing home?"

"Never!" Eva screeches. "They tie people in bed in those places. And tell you what to do all the time." She is adamant. If anyone tries to take her, she'll swallow a fistful of pills and that will be the end of it. Pfftt.

While Eva wobbles around the kitchen fixing a pot of tea, Claire sits on the sofa massaging her temples. "I don't know what to do for her," she says. "To tell you the truth. I'd be all for leaving her here to die in her own space. Even if she fell, or had a heart attack alone at night, she'd have done it her way. But you just can't let her burn the place down and take everyone else with her." No one can force Eva into a home. She knows that's the law and she counts on it. "The only way they can take me is if they prove I'm senile. And I'm not. So that's that."

After her daughter leaves, Eva explains how things work in a nursing home: You have to eat when they want you to eat. You can't stay up late and watch TV. They cut your hair whether you want it cut or not. "The nurses make all the women look like bobcats in those places."

Eva spits a little as she talks. She uses a hanky to dry her lips. After a while she calms down, snaps on the TV, stares at it blankly for a few minutes, then turns it off. "Nothing good on. I like the talk shows. A person can learn a lot from them."

Eva gets most of her information from TV. She stopped taking the newspaper when she could no longer read it. She can't see the TV very well either, but she can listen. She hears stories about old people eating dog food. About muggers. And rapists. And children who quit caring about their parents.

"I'm lucky. I have plenty of food. My family still comes to visit. I'm not afraid of robbers." But there are three locks on the hallway door. Each one is bolted.

Eva swears she never takes a nap. She yawns, dozes in the peacock-patterned chair, awakens patting the mussed edges of her hair. "I must have dozed off. That's very unusual for me. Would you bring me my hairbrush?"

The bathroom smells of talc and mint mouthwash. Eva's underwear hangs over a ceramic towel rod. The cleaned white shoes sit on the windowsill, drying in the sun. A blue nylon nightgown, trimmed in lace, hangs on the bathroom door.

Eva brushes her hair. She preens, pulling its thickness down past her waist. "Not many women my age have hair like this," she says. "When I was younger it was the color of mahogany. But it has been gray a long time now. You know, in a nursing home they'd cut it, right here at the nape."

A CROWN OF BRAIDS

In spite of the lovely day, Gram was not happy with me. I took her to a place she didn't want to go. Hundreds of times before, she insisted we drive to Jack Lake. It was full of memories for her. She would talk and talk and talk. The fish. The sound of the Whippoorwills. The night the bear came to the window. The people who came and went – friends and relatives swimming in the lake. Towels and wet suits on the clothesline.

This day was different. Gram didn't want to talk. Didn't want to have anything to do with the place. In the afternoon we would go to the Antigo nursing home, check her in. I would leave her there. I didn't want to do this. I'm sure she didn't either, but she had insisted. She had called me in Milwaukee.

"You need to come up here. Now. I need you to help me pack." I had to write her name on her pretty lace nightgowns and see that her dishes went to the health aide's daughter. She left her favorite ceramic bluebird on the buffet. I could take it someplace tomorrow, she said. She didn't care.

The car ride was spontaneous. Or maybe it was just a habit. We'd been together so many years I felt as if I could read her. But of course, I could not. This was new territory for her, to stop fighting against the end of her life and do what? Embrace it? I don't think she ever did that. She did, at least, decide to run the show herself. If she went into the nursing home on her own, no one was forcing her. She would not be told what to do.

When the packing was nearly done, she told me to get her hairbrush. I undid her braids – they were long and wound enough around her head to form a beautiful crown.

Would I brush her hair? Of course. Her little blue rocker had been lost along the way; the kitchen chair would have to do.

She sat tall. In her mid-nineties, her body, like her hair, still looked full and strong. If this was today instead of the 1980s when you either lived with your youngers or in a nursing home, she'd have more choices. She might even have a part time job bossing people around. Gram was good at that.

Well into the brushing, she said to get the camera. On this, her last day "at home," she wanted a shot of her hair hanging down her back, below her waist – which was still smaller than the rest of her.

That was the second thing she was proud of. Her figure. She tucked in the waist of every dress, every coat, she ever owned. If you've got a good thing, why not show it?

Her face looked old, but nowhere near as old as she was. And she was lucky, the aides at the home did not cut it. She died with her hair done up in braids.

THE PLACE HE LOVED

My feet are pushing hard on the pedals. This is a new bike, my first. Mom, Dad, and Uncle Warren are standing on the front steps watching. My feet slip. The pedals spin. I fly backwards down the hill, over the curb, and under a moving car.

I feel Dad's hands on my ankles as he pulls me out from under the car. My face is wet. I hear Mom crying. Minutes later, Dad is racing to the hospital. Warren is in the back seat, holding me. My head is wrapped so I can't see, but I can hear his mellow voice, "It's okay, Judy. You're going to be okay."

The next day, my head still bandaged, I wake up early and find Warren snoozing on the living room floor. He's curled with a pillow and soft summer blanket. I cuddle in next to him and stay there – feel the warmth, listen to him breathe, watch the dust dance in the sunlight.

In a year or two my parent's marriage will end. The sister who teaches my 4th grade class at Holy Angels elementary school says having divorced parents is a sin, and some of my classmates' parents agree. The kids chase me to the brick apartment building where I live with my mom and big sister. I yell up at the second-story window. "Uncle Warren! Uncle Warren!" I know he can't hear me. He's way far away, fighting a war. The kids back off and I feel safe. Uncle Warren does that for me, even when he's far away.

My uncle's parents were also divorced, and he also moved from place to place, always the outsider. He was born during a thunderstorm to Eva and Holgar Rasmussen, whose marriage was as wild as the weather. Eva had two boys from her first marriage – Roy, the oldest, and my dad, Lionel. And a daughter, Claire, who became Warren's "little mother."

Eva gave up on her second marriage when Warren was in fourth grade. She sent Claire to live with a well-to-do family that needed help, and Warren to live with his grandparents in a logging camp up north. In winter he walked through snowy woods to a one room schoolhouse in a teeny town called Kopenick. He swept his grandfather's blacksmith shop. And in summer, he picked buckets of wild raspberries.

When Eva had enough money to take care of Warren, she took him back to Appleton, where mother and son lived until he was 13 and times got hard again. With no home and no money, they returned once more to the north woods and lived at Jack Lake in a ramshackle cottage Claire purchased on land contract. For two years, Warren and Eva ate fish, potatoes, berries, and deer meat.

In the winter, they chopped holes in the ice to get water.

Despite the hardship, Jack Lake was the place Warren loved best of all. He had a girlfriend, the niece of the only other family on the lake. Her parents sent her there to keep her away from boys. It didn't work very well. Warren swam across the lake to be with her.

When Claire came home for a visit, brother and sister swam to the middle of the lake and floated for hours, pretending they didn't know their mother was standing on the rocky shore yoo-hooing them to come in.

They became more of a family after they moved back to Appleton. Claire taught her little brother how to dance. They won prizes at local competitions. He went to high school and was the first boy in the family to graduate. To celebrate, his brother Lionel drove up from Milwaukee with a brand-new suit for him to wear on his big day.

Over the years, things also improved at Jack Lake. The cottage got a new roof and became a vacation place for the family. We fished and swam and picked berries. Uncle Warren showed me the best place to hide from grownups – lying flat on the roof of the outhouse. After dinner, he and I would pour gravy on slices of Gram's homemade bread and stand at the shoreline, listening to the loons call at sunset.

He joined the Army. Then the Air Force. He sent me a bombardier patch I imagined he'd worn. I got mom to sew it on a blue plaid shirt I wore until the collar frayed and then stashed in my bottom drawer, under my jeans.

While I was being his "bombardier" he was serving in World War II, Korea, and Viet Nam, becoming a Chief Warrant Officer, and earning a Bronze Star.

By the time he came back to the states for good, Aunt Claire had sold the cottage. Warren and I walked the property, trespassing, though it felt as if we still had rights to it. The trees had grown tall enough to hide the outhouse. Each of the new owner's kids had built their own little cabin. They were all falling apart. Critters ran in and out. The place was a shambles.

The last time I saw my Uncle Warren, we both knew he was near the end. The Parkinson's was so advanced he could barely walk, but when they turned up the music in the rehab unit, he gave me a look that said, "Let's dance." The therapist gripped his waist belt and off we went, the three of us shuffling a passable two step. I could feel the music sink into him and feel the last little bits of his warmth. Later, when it was quiet, he put his hand on mine and said: "Scatter my ashes in Jack Lake."

The ice is off the lake. I paddle a canoe out to the middle and imagine that below the surface, the water holds memories of every person who ever swam or fished there – especially the skinny kid who knew where he could catch a nice bass.

The canoe drifts to his favorite cove, the one where he felt most peaceful, where the reeds grew tall and he said, "No one knows I'm here." I trail my fingers in the water and give Warren back to the place he loved.

It was a day like so many we shared.

AUNT CLAIRE SLIPPING AWAY

Aunt Claire holding the dolly her daddy sent to her for Christmas. He was in a TB sanitarium out west at the time.

Do sit down. The green chair is quite comfortable. It's mine, from my home. The paintings are mine, too. The Gibson Girls are especially nice. Marvin said they remind him of me.

Can you see the birds from there? They come every day, eat when I eat. They're such good company, like old friends come to visit.

No, I wasn't sleeping, just curled up in a daydream, picking berries with my Gram. When I wear her scarf, I can smell her sweet, berry smell. With Gram, there was no two ways about it, you either picked your share or you didn't get to eat.

Mother lived in Appleton then, with the boys. I lived with a wealthy family, keeping house, babysitting. Dad was in a TB San out west. He died there when I was still a kid.

Would you like a piece of candy? I like the dark chocolate. It's good for you, you know. I used to be a nurse. Well, a nurses aide. Then, a hairdresser. I was going to open my own shop when I met Marvin. He changed all that.

Dear Marvin. Fifty-five years and never a dust-up.

I bet you don't fight either, do you?

I didn't think so. People fight too much. They should learn to get along. Of course, you couldn't fight with Marvin if you tried.

I wasn't ready for, you know, *that,* when we got married. He said he'd wait. We drove to Pennsylvania so he could work on the Turnpike. They were building it then, blasting through rock, paving the roads. He ran the crews.

Claire's darling Marvin, out with the road crews, building the PA Turnpike from Pennsylvania to Kansas.

One night I went up to our room in the boarding house and found a box tied with a huge peach-colored bow. Inside, a soft, flowing nightgown, the most beautiful thing I'd ever seen. There were apple blossoms on the tree outside our window.

That was our first time.

We followed the interstate west, little green trailer to live in, farmyards, outhouses, quilts on the clotheslines. Got to know a lot of people in a lot of places. I opened a few shops along the way. A little French boutique. A corner antique shop. I also restored old houses, but we always left them behind.

When Marvin was getting ready to retire, I built a house in the country. Big windows overlooking Bear Lake. It was meant to be a summer place, but we loved it so much we moved in and lived there. We had roots, finally. Gardens full of roots – beans, berries, potatoes, grapes for wine.

And an apple tree.

All the years after Marvin passed on, I sat in the window and watched that tree.

Spring blossoms.

Winter snows.

The little wood bench he made for us to sit on turned muddy grey and tilted in the ground.

There are things you never get over in this life.

I barely remember my home now. It seems I've been here so long. I don't know why I'm here, but the doctor said I can't go home. He said I might live forever because I did everything right. Didn't drink. Didn't smoke. Didn't sleep around.

I'm old now. Nearly two hundred. I get around okay. In the middle of the night when everyone's asleep, I get up and walk the halls, past the night sounds of people snoring. There's one sad soul who cries all night.

Last week I had lunch with the Queen. She wanted to say thanks to me for saving one of her horses. It was being chased by a bear. I drove alongside the horse and stopped it from galloping into traffic.

The Queen was grateful. She's quite partial to horses, you know.

A little boy brings animals for me to pet – a rabbit, a frog, a snake. I pet, of course, and then he says, "Lady, would you like to kiss it?" I was a little nervous about kissing the snake, but you know what? It wasn't altogether unpleasant.

I've decided not to marry the pilot. He flies by my window, tips his wings, waves. He can see me here in bed. One time he dropped a rock out of the airplane window. There was a note attached. The nurse read it for me, said it was a proposal. Imagine that. A proposal. What would I want with that?

I already had the best. My Marvin.

Fifty-five years and never a dust-up.

I bet you don't fight either, do you? People fight too much. They should learn to get along.

Of course, you couldn't fight with Marvin if you tried.

Claire and Marvin Peterson, happy to be together, flowers tumbling alongside the house they loved. They left the house to me. And always always welcomed me "home." My favorite memory is of Claire on a ladder, writing a poem on the living room wall. She painted over it. When I asked where she had her poems written, she said, "In the walls. The house loves them."

BEAN SOUP

My brother lives thousands of miles away from me in Alaska, where he built a successful business while his wife raised the children. Brother and I were close as kids. Not so close during the busy, middle, years. And now good friends again. Except for politics, where he is The Great White Hunter and I'm The Bra Burner.

I never actually burned a bra. And he doesn't hunt anymore. Still, we are far Left, far Right – the difference that's torn so many friends and families apart. Especially when our whole country is on one side or the other and the sides are more likely to spit at each other than talk over the fence.

Trouble is, the madness goes on. Literally.

A few months ago, my brother asked me where I stood. He knew he was surrounded by people who thought his way. He also knew I thought differently and respected me enough to ask the question. We tried, both of us. We knew that once upon a time we could talk and come to consensus. Not anymore. Our language had become loaded. Sentences we thought were neutral carried unwitting attempts to convince.

We swore off politics. Conversations became thinner, and less frequent.

One day I found a photo of us when we were young, and the biggest argument we had was who'd beat who in a bike race.

I posted the photo on Facebook with the following comment: "The love we share is deeper than the distance between us. This photo was taken the year after my mom married his dad and we got each other in the bargain. Politically, we're miles apart, but we'd each take a bullet for the other."

That opened the door again. For a while.

More recently, I sent him a note: "Let's not let politics stand in the way of love. How about we plan to connect at least once a week?"

He agreed. Now our conversations go something like this.

Me: I made a pot of bean soup today. Want some?

Bro: I'd love a bowl. It's 9 degrees up here.

That's it, plus updates on his antique autos and my book sales.

Will either of us switch sides? Probably not. But we have cleared a path so we can walk together. There is kindness. There is love. There is hope. And a big bubbling pot of bean soup.

THE GIRL NEXT DOOR

A lady my mom works with gives me a diary for Christmas. It's one of those little books with a flower on the cover and a lock that opens with a tiny gold key: My Diary. I plan to use it. I'll write about the new school in Cleveland, the friends I'm making, the shoes the other girls are wearing. I'll write everything in My Diary.

Mom says that might not be so wise. "What if someone reads it?" That makes me wonder how much she knows about me and Jerry Oriel.

I throw the diary away.

A few years later, I'm living in Milwaukee with my dad and stepmother. The girl next door is my best friend. She keeps a journal – that's fancy for a diary that doesn't have a lock and key. She writes everything in her journal, and I decide to give that a try.

It isn't long before the cleaning lady finds my writing and shows it to my stepmother, who has a fit. I still hadn't gone that far with anybody so that wasn't the issue. It was that my grades were lousy, and Sister Beatrix said I need to quit writing all the time and pay attention to my studies.

So I'm grounded. Again.

My friend keeps writing everything in her journal. She says she plans to do that all her life. I wonder if that's so wise.

I go to boarding school. Graduate. Get married. Get unmarried. Move out east where life takes on a whole new complexion with bigger jobs, part time college and fancier parties. I write at the university, but it's mostly fiction and mostly I throw it away, even if I get a good grade. I decide not to marry the lawyer. I do marry the Navy corpsman who turns into a broker, and I start writing to keep a lid on life. The foster kids. The community projects. The travel. The breakup. I go on for pages, notebooks, writing most when I'm sad. Wondering where I went wrong. Would I ever get things right?

The journaling keeps up through the move to Chicago, to San Francisco, and finally back home to Wisconsin.

My friend and I meet up again. She's still journaling. Has, all her life. Through marriage. Five kids. Falling crazy in love with her son's best friend. Fighting it for a couple years and still ending up in an affair. Her husband finds her journal in the trunk of her car and that's that. She's out of the marriage, and out of the affair. But the passion is so deep for both her and the young man that they keep finding each other, unable to resist. I was at their wedding in an odd little backyard chapel in January, so cold we all kept our coats on. The bride and groom didn't seem to be cold. Her two sons walked her down the straw covered aisle. Her three girls were there. I, and surely others of the guests, wondered how it could come to this and how it would end.

The thing is, it didn't end. They've been married for over 30 years. She is forgetful now, and he is the most devoted caregiver I've ever seen.

I don't get to visit her as often as I'd like, but I send cards every week. They usually include a little writing about something we did when we were kids, before we got to be 80 and had clearly gone "that far," cried that hard, and loved that deeply. Her husband sends a text after showing her the cards. He tells me how she reacted, which is generally pleased. But she doesn't remember that her mom's parakeet squealed on her when she came home late. She does remember us tanning – lying on towels in the back yard, bodies soaked in baby oil tinted brown with iodine. I don't know if she remembers us sitting on her front steps, sharing the important things we wrote in our journals.

Perhaps my mom was right when she saw me with that first little diary. My friend certainly paid a high price for her writing. And yet, in the end, it came out fine. Her kids and grandkids are grown. They love her and her husband. One day, probably after she passes, they'll read what she wrote in her journals and be in awe of the amazing life she led.

As for me, I quit journaling when I started writing for a living. I still think it's a good idea. But I also still worry about someone else reading it. Not that I care about the personal stuff. We all have that. It's more because of the dreary days when I filled the pages with whining. I imagine a stranger sitting in a rocking chair on a wide front porch, shaking her head, thinking, "This poor girl never had a good day in her life." And that would be so untrue.

Jean and I on our way to march on Washington. So many memories.

FOLLOWING SISTER LOURDETTE

The Marian Center, formerly St. Mary's Academy. The Sisters of St. Francis of Assisi founded Cardinal Stritch College and many other educational artistic ventures in these buildings. The top floor, right side, was home to Redbird Studio for 25 years.

Looking at a photo of the old St. Mary's Academy takes me back to one prophetic day in 1992, when I walked past the front of the building and thought, if I could have a tiny room up there on the top floor, I could write a book.

Sister Lourdette Van Driel lead me up the stairs. If you have ever followed Lourdette upstairs, you know that this was a quick trip. She showed me a tiny room in the northeast corner that had more square feet of window than of floor. From my little perch I could see over the trees to Lake Michigan, and over the Hoan bridge to downtown Milwaukee.

My only near neighbors on the top floor were a Montessori Training Center, and an artist who thought it would be cool if we rented an empty room down the hall to hold workshops. I thought that was a dumb idea but did it anyway. That turned into Redbird Studio writing center and 25 of the best years of my life.

My first plan was to offer one small critique group, something welcoming, supportive, more structured than a living room group and more practical than most of my grad level workshops.

Two people came the first day.

Within a few months, we had eighty-five people in the Social Room for a conference called "The Best Writers' Workshop in the World." Someone at *Writers Digest* magazine called to ask what made our workshop the best. We – three or four writer friends and I – outlined a plan that included a keynote speaker, the editor of *Reader's Digest* magazine.

The night before the workshop, when the editor was on her way to Milwaukee, she received a call that her father was dying. Obviously, she went to him. And obviously, we had a problem. Maximum registration. Four breakout rooms set up. Luncheon prepared. And no keynote speaker.

That was a long night. At the very last minute an agent friend stepped in and saved the day.

After that, we grew as quickly as we could and still stay focused. "We" meant me, my husband Dave, and all the wonderful people who were gracious enough to help. Together, we grew from one roundtable a week to four, from a single special event to a calendar filled with seminars like "Blood, Guts and the Murder Scene," "Writers' Boot Camp," and a weeklong program of "Writing for Social Change."

Some of the events changed us. On "The Great Train Write," we went to Chicago, wrote in the Great Hall in Union Station, and toured Newberry Library – where they let us hold books that were older than this country.

After lunch, we got on a city bus headed for Graceland Cemetery. A couple of the writers looked like they were getting nervous, especially when some boisterous teenagers got on the bus with us and started fooling around. I think the kids saw what was up and had mercy because they signaled each other to start singing. Turned out it was a chorus of gospel singers. They rocked the bus all the way to Graceland, and I am absolutely certain that they warmed a few hearts.

A 1996 issue of *The Redbird Review* contained stories and articles by our writers, and a schedule of current programs: Roundtable groups for novelists, published writers, poets, and writers in general. An Intro to Novel Writing and Intro to Acting. Meet the Editor. Meet the Agent. Reading for Writers. Journal Writing. Business Writing. Writing for Children. A Room of One's Own (for women writers), The Devil's Workshop (at Parfrey's Glen), the Second Annual Performance Night, and a Hike Write.

The Hike Write was notable because the Milwaukee Journal Sentinel took photos of us hiking and writing at Scuppernong Springs, and spread them, full color, on the front page of the Good Morning section.

The next day, the principal of Riley Elementary School called asking me to work with his students. The first thing out of my mouth was, "I don't do kids." So, he had me spend a day with the teachers. Then the teachers took me into their classrooms to show me how what we did that day worked with the kids, and together we created a plan to get a school full of city kids as interested in writing as they were in basketball.

A couple of years into that first student program, kids at the school were heard calling out in the halls, "Hey! Do you get to go to Redbird this year?"

That was probably my greatest success. And fondest memory.

In 2011, I published *Shut Up & Write!* – a book that contains much of what I learned from all the people who taught and took classes and otherwise supported Redbird Studio. It does exactly what I hoped it would do, helps writers get through the long haul.

Everyone who writes knows it isn't a one-day deal. You learn craft, you write for a while, you come back and learn more about the craft. *Shut Up & Write!* is there for the beginning, and the comeback.

The gala night at The Marian Center, celebrating the release of the well-loved *Shut Up & Write!* It's still fun to see all these familiar faces.

THE MORTADELLA LADY

Mom didn't have many choices when she was young. She was one of ten kids in a dirt-poor family that lived on potatoes and dreams. Her dad was a carpenter who also started one of the first moving companies in Milwaukee. He must have made some money doing that, but it doesn't seem the family saw much of it.

Mom had to quit school in fifth or sixth grade and work full time to help the family. That really wasn't all that unusual at that time – the early 1920s. But she loved school. All her life, she took every chance she got to attend classes, here and there, on any topic. Mostly, she loved English classes, and writing. No one was more thrilled than my mother that I earned a master's degree and wrote for a living. I could almost see her living in that dream.

In the early 1980s we bought a house together. She wanted to move back to Milwaukee, Stepdad wanted to stay in Florida. She got her head up one day and told him she was coming back and that was that. He decided to come along. We bought a two-story Milwaukee bungalow. They lived downstairs. Dave and I lived up. For several years we threw our laundry drown the chute and it came back up folded.

Later, as mom and dad needed help, we spent more time downstairs. It was at that point – on a day when she was a little irked with me – that I gave her the two binders so she could write her day-to-day. One would be a good place to scream at me when she was angry. I promised not to read it, not even after she died. The other notebook was for her memories. Reading that, I fell in love with The Mortadella Lady, the way my mother saw her and the world around her.

I read this story of hers at a Redbird author event. She was in the audience. I have a photo of her, taken while the applause was ringing in her ears.

The Mortadella Lady

By Marge Kiefert, Miller, Weyenberg, Bakic

When I was about eleven years old, we lived in a house next to a large apartment building. There was a lady who lived in one of the apartments on the top floor. She took a shine to me and always called me when she saw me playing in the field next to her building. She would have me get her groceries for her. She was a beautiful Irish woman with the prettiest blue eyes. I can see her yet sitting in the chair in her kitchen making up the grocery list. She would put the pencil in her mouth and twirl it around, wetting the point before she put down another item. She seemed to be looking out in space as she was recalling what she needed. I used to sit there watching her and waiting, thinking how wonderful and pretty she was. I got so I could remember her grocery list without her writing it down.

She would have me get Mortadella and Danish. I only knew about sausage and schnecks. I felt like a millionaire's daughter, doing her shopping. Our family couldn't afford Mortadella or Danish pastries.

She had a beautiful piano. I remember her playing and singing, "Chicago, Chicago, That Tuddely Town. They do things, they say things in Chicago..." I can't remember any more of it, but I enjoyed hearing her play and sing. Seemed like it brought back some old memories for her.

She was from Chicago. She was separated from her husband. He lived at the Republican Hotel on Third Street in Milwaukee. It was a hotel where wealthy businessmen resided. She would visit him there; he never came to her apartment. She seemed very happy on the days she visited with him. I don't think they ever had any children, as she never talked of any. Guess he must have supported her, as she didn't work out. There was a man that came to visit her and stayed overnight once in a while. She told me he was her brother. I remember his name was Tom.

Then there was another man that would visit. I remember they used to go into her bedroom and stay there for a while. Guess I was too young to realize what was going on. One time they took me with them to a tavern they went to. There were booths and a bar and we sat down in one of the booths. They ordered beers for themselves and a soda for me. I thought that was wonderful. In a little while they went off someplace in another room and left me sitting there. After a while they came back, we went home. Never thought anything wrong about that until years after.

The Mortadella Lady used to tell fortunes with cards. There was another woman in the building that taught her how and they used to lay out the cards together. I remember the red Queen was a lady coming into your life. Heart, love. Black cards meant trouble. Diamonds, money. And the Ace of Spades, death. Once she read the cards for me. Can't remember much, but she did say I would marry and have money late in life. She read palms too. She said my lifeline showed I would live long.

She left a key for me so I could go into the apartment if she wasn't there and do a little cleaning for her. Sometimes I would swipe fruit or cookies. I wonder what she would have done had she caught me? I know it was stealing, but we didn't get much in goodies at home. My mother had all she could do to have three meals for a family of ten at that time. My sisters, Ethel and Lillian, were born later.

Years after, I saw my friend on the streetcar. The streetcar ran on Third Street at that time. It was a trolly car with a conductor in front who did the steering, and one in the back who collected the fares: five cents. You got on at the rear and left from the front. I was shocked to see how much she had changed. She was drunk and ragged – unkempt, like a bag lady, mumbling out loud She didn't recognize me, and I didn't talk to her. That was the last I saw of her. Seems so sad, she was such a wonderful, intelligent, beautiful person. I often wonder what happened to her to make her turn out that way.

ROSES FOR MOTHER

The first roses I gave my mother came from Holy Cross Cemetery. They were in a big bouquet with a pink "Mother" ribbon that didn't thrill her quite as much as I thought it would.

That's when I learned that you're supposed to be nice to dead people. Don't take their flowers. Don't step on their graves. Be polite and honor those who have "gone before."

That started me on a lifelong habit of paying attention to the ways we honor the dead. I wander cemeteries. Read obits. I actually get out of my car to read inscriptions on roadside monuments. It can take me hours to drive to the next town, but I love the things I see and what they say about us.

I especially like old cemeteries like Forest Home. It was one of the Milwaukee's first garden-like cemeteries and has been a resting place of the city's elite since the mid-1800s. There you see fancy stones and huge crypts for people like city founder and mayor Byron Kilbourn, scientist and founder of the U.S. Weather Bureau Increase Lapham, meat packer John Plankinton, and beer baron Joseph Schlitz. The Blatz family has a mausoleum that looks like a small church.

But for all the famous names, the monuments to ordinary people are the ones that catch your heart. In Section 45, there's a tall, white hand-carved relief picturing a large man and, to his left and in a much smaller scale, an older woman. The stone was carved by Edward Lieber to honor his parents: Karl, who died at 43 in 1869, and Anna, who died at 84 in 1905. Edward chiseled it after his mother's death and did it so carefully that over 100 years later, you can still see the straw in his father's hat and the eyelet on his mother's dress.

Among the massive angels, urns and obelisks, there is a tiny marble cot marking the grave of an infant – blanket pulled aside, a dent in the stone pillow says, "this child has gone away." It reminds me of my little brother. Mark was just eight months old when he died of congenital heart disease. The year was 1956. Had it been a few years later, he might have been saved. I've lost a photo that I took of him, propped up on Gram's lap, wrapped in a cozy blanket. His eyes were the most striking thing in the photo. He looked as if he knew everything that was going on, who was there to take care, and how long it would last. Wisdom, I think you'd say. A kind of wisdom we who run around all day do not attain. It takes quiet, and a warm blanket, to know all that a baby knows.

I wonder about the little one who lies under the marble blanket. I'd like to think he and Mark have found a nice place to play. Without realizing it, we become connected with the people who are memorialized in cemeteries and public places.

Milwaukee once had a "bridge to nowhere" – originally planned as part of the freeway system but stopped in response to local opposition. Now it's known as the Hoan bridge. It was named for Mayor Daniel Hoan, a man who opposed any type of lakefront development. During the depression, Daniel Hoan cut his own pay to create funding for a jobs program, but he didn't get memorialized for that.

On a much smaller scale, there is a boulder on the corner of Superior and Russell in Bay View that honors members of a labor movement who were killed there May 5, 1886, when they marched with 1500 others on the Milwaukee Iron Co. Rolling Mill, protesting for an eight-hour workday. When Governor Jeremiah Rusk (of Rusk Street) heard they were coming, he said, "Fire on them." The militia shot and killed at least five men (the records are unclear) including a schoolboy who was in the crowd and a man who was watching from his backyard nearby.

It's to our credit, I think, that we also memorialize lighthearted events. In 1945 a mallard captivated the city when she laid her eggs on a piling below the Wisconsin Avenue bridge. War-tired citizens the world over watched as Gertie the Duck nursed her little family. I was one of the lucky kids whose mom took us to stand along the railing near Gertie's nest. Today, a sculpture of Gertie and two of her ducklings (Dee Dee and Pee Wee) sits on a platform on the bridge. An inscription says she "represented new life and hope."

In 1910, Richard D. Whitehead, the first superintendent of the Wisconsin Humane Society, erected a tribute to his pets on the comer of Bow Street and 16th Street (renamed to honor national Hispanic activist, Cesar E. Chavez). The monument – originally a horse watering trough – was later used as a fountain and then a planter. It was built by Whitehead, "In remembrance of my faithful friends: Horse: George. Dogs: Dandy, Pet, Punch, Judy & Shorty. Cats: Frank & Henry. Birds: Browney & Dick."

I admire Whitehead's choice of names for his animals, particularly the dogs Punch and Judy.

When an artist friend lost her son, she hand carved her thoughts on a boulder from the family cottage. My sister honored her son, (who always did the Christmas trimming,) by decorating a large outdoor tree in her yard. Others wrote books, or stitched patchwork "memory" quilts.

As I look at the memorials I favor now, I see a common thread, an urge for life in them, a symbolism quite different than gravestones that say, "This life has ended."

I seem to be looking for the ones that say, from deep inside us, "this life goes on."

MOM'S BICYCLE

When Mom was 76 years old, she learned to ride a two-wheeled bicycle. She and Dad lived in Vero Beach, Florida at the time. Most of her friends in Village Green used three-wheelers to get to the pool and rec center. Mom had a three-wheeler too, but she'd always wanted to ride a "re-al" bike.

So she bought one. She went to the bike shop, purchased a full-sized two-wheeler, and told the bike guy to put training wheels on it. Then she pedaled around the subdivision until she got the training wheels off, and then she called everyone she knew to say, "Guess what I did!"

A few years later, when she was living back in Milwaukee, she wanted to brush up on her skills. By then, the Florida bike was looking pretty tall to her. So, she shopped garage sales and bought a short one with a banana seat. Then she asked me to go out in the alley with her to practice.

Picture this. Mom's on a banana seat bike. I'm running alongside her, panting like mad. The neighbors are bending over their garbage cans, laughing at us. One guy shouts, "I can see which one of you is in the best shape!"

I growl at him, "Yeah, and she's 84 years old."

Mom shoots me a look – you know the kind – and says, "I am not! I'm only eighty-three!" She was only eighty-three. And when she died, she was only eighty- seven.

If you think she's sitting on a cloud, strumming a harp, you're wrong. She's up there riding a bicycle. And I'm here to tell you, St. Peter better get the hell out of the way.

Mom and I on the grass slope leading down to Bay View beach. I may have been reminding her how she and the other aunts took us kids to Bradford beach in the summer. The wet smell of the ladies' changing room. The sailors who followed her up the stairs. She denied that. "Oh, Judy. That never happened." Oh, yes it did!

ACKNOWLEDGEMENTS

It is a given. I will write my gratitude to the village, then spend all kinds of time thinking of people I forgot to mention.

As usual, I say, "It takes a Village." Many notable people have said this, but that doesn't lessen the truth of it. Writers start with a thought, struggle to find words for it, struggle again (and again) to get the words in the right order. Then there are editors and agents, and people who help with marketing and distribution. By this time dozens of hands have worked on the brilliant idea and the writer is wondering, Is it good? Was it ever any good?

Well, let's hope this book is good. And if it is, here are some of the dozens of people who helped it become so.

Dave Blank: Husband. For patience, spelling, peanut butter cookies, and a glorious website. The Blank Family: For welcoming me into the herd. Bob Bakic: My Big Brother. For shoving me off the dime on this writing journey. I'll miss him forever.

Lynn Lance, Carol Storniolo, Mary Merryfield: The Weyenberg girls – I'm proud to be their sister. Janese Wills: First Niece. First Godchild. First baby to love.

Mary Lou Bell: Best friend. Reminds me I'm good at this. So is she. Christi Craig: Publisher. Accepted numerous final versions - and fixed them. Shauna Singh Baldwin: Excellent novels, excellent friend. Always knows which way is up. Elaine Bergstrom: Part of the show since the first hullabaloo. Annie Chase: An Ace from critique to car repair. Aleta Chossek: Writes, gives feedback, brings Meru coffee to every occasion.

Christi Clancy: I knew right off she'd be a star. Sharon Nesbit Davis: Makes the hardest stories worth holding on to and reading again. Maura Fitzgerald: Such good company, such good writing. Mackenzie Harris: Put the blue glass in the fire. Get in the canoe. Mac is on her way. Beth Huwiler: She writes way above my head, and I'm always eager to read it. Kathy Lanzarotti: Creates the most surprising plots and characters. Laura

Lentz: Oh, to write like Laura. A mutual admiration society. Pat Lorenz: Here from the beginning. Funny presentations and buckets of Chicken Soup.

Valerie Menges: Knows all the right words – not an easy task in my crowd. Judy McKee: Has mastered the science of making people smile. No. Laugh. Out loud. Katie Miller: Clear thinking and a warm heart I've come to rely on. Marjorie Pagel: So so good at spreading news to help her fellow writers. Kim Parsons: Prose and poetry – on a hiking trail or in a canoe. Sara Rattan: Great friend and writer. Pulls me back from the brink with her brilliant critique. Joanne Riordan: Asked to read an early draft. And I was so so happy to let her. Anne Rooney: You name it, she's been there. And helped a million people along the way. Joanne Rooney: Writer, Speaker, Swimmer, a powerhouse on legs. Jeannée Sacken: Never saw a writer work so hard and do it so well.

Mary Rooney Sheahen: Besides being beautiful, she loans her sister to us from time to time. Kim Suhr: Turned Redbird into Redoak, making it better than it's ever been. Robert Vaughan: Great teacher and writer. He bends all the right genres. Amy Waldman: Smart. Well grounded. I turn to her for insight on the toughest of topics. Carolyn

Kott Washburne: There's nothing quite like being nestled into an article she's written. Jonathan West: Rimmed glasses and bow ties, he is personality with a capital P. I love him. Carol Wobig: Kind of shy. Kind of phenomenal. Writes the pants off of the best stories.

Judy Bridges was years into a career writing speeches and marketing programs when she realized she really loves to teach and founded Redbird Studio. She spent the next 25 years helping people find the words they want to say. The first lines of many books and shorter works were written and polished in workshops she led in the studio, on woodland trails, in cemeteries, on trains and city buses. When an elementary school principal asked her to work with his students, she said, "I don't do kids." That turned into school year and summer programs for youth of all ages and backgrounds. When teaching, Judy looks in each person for the thing they love, the thing they can build on. No writing is insignificant. The obituary is as important as the novel. When she wrote *Shut Up & Write!* readers said it was as much about life as about writing. In her memoir, *It Didn't Start Out That Way*, she brings her own life to the page.

BOOKS, ACCOLADES, & PREVIOUS PUBLICATIONS BY JUDY BRIDGES

Shut Up & Write! Published by Redbird Studio Press, 2011. Winner of four national awards, including *Foreword Reviews* Book of the Year, and praised by the editor of *The Writer Magazine*. September 2011.

"The Price of Independence." Winner of Milwaukee Press Club Department of Mass Communication "Best Feature Award" and published in *Milwaukee Journal Insight*. November 28, 1982.

"The Train Goes Both Ways." Awarded "Best Short Story" and published in *Wisconsin Woman Magazine*. August 1987.

"The Place He Loved." Published in *Milwaukee Magazine*. August 2014.

"Bean Soup." Read on air at WUWM 89.7 National Public Radio *Wisconsin Life*, and published on WUWM website with subtitle, "Navigating politics with family." January 2021.

"Roses for Mother" published in *Milwaukee Magazine*. June 2001.

Named "Woman Who Put Her Stamp On Milwaukee" by the Milwaukee Postal Service.

Winner (2 years), Wauwatosa Village Playhouse for *Downtown at the La De Da* and *Bag of Bones.*

SOURCES

Excerpt in "The Shoebox" from the poem "Lines to a Little Girl" by Ruth Mary DuBois, first printed in *Ladies Home Journal*, during the 1940s. (Note: Clipping found in Marge Bakic's shoebox of memories.)

Except in "Mortadella Lady" from a journal entry by Marge Bakic, written in the 1990s.

www.ingramcontent.com/pod-product-compliance
Lightning Source LLC
Chambersburg PA
CBHW040521170726
48295CB00012B/288

* 9 7 8 1 7 3 6 5 5 1 9 6 7 *